W. J Spry

Bishop Colenso and the Descent of Jacob into Egypt

An Analysis

W. J Spry

Bishop Colenso and the Descent of Jacob into Egypt
An Analysis

ISBN/EAN: 9783337237509

Printed in Europe, USA, Canada, Australia, Japan

Cover: Foto ©Lupo / pixelio.de

More available books at **www.hansebooks.com**

Bishop Colenso and the Pentateuch,

PART I.

BISHOP COLENSO

AND THE

DESCENT OF JACOB INTO EGYPT:

An Analysis:

By W. J. SPRY.

ENTERED AT STATIONERS' HALL.

LONDON:
WERTHEIM, MACINTOSH, AND HUNT,
PATERNOSTER ROW AND HOLLES STREET.
EDINBURGH: JOHN MENZIES, HANOVER STREET.
MANCHESTER: JOHN HEYWOOD. DUBLIN: M'GLASHAN & GILL.
DEVONPORT: JOHN R. H. SPRY, TAVISTOCK STREET.

PRICE TWO SHILLINGS.

BISHOP COLENSO
AND
THE PENTATEUCH.

PART I.

PREFACE.

Two years have not yet elapsed since the religious world in this protestant country was startled from its slumbers by the rapid circulation of a volume known as "Essays and Reviews," in which (amongst others) a Professor of Hebrew, a Parochial Clergyman, and a Regius Professor of Greek had united in their efforts to overturn the basis of the faith of millions, and to raise doubts in the minds of those who were unable to examine the Jewish and Christian Scriptures in their originals. Ere the agitation thus occasioned has been allayed, and while the public mind is still in suspense as to what may be the decision of the law-courts on the questions which have been submitted in connexion therewith, a violent commotion has been raised, and a great public scandal occasioned, by a Bishop of the Church of England having published a work, wherein the Deity of our Lord is insidiously set aside and his knowledge declared to be limited, while Moses's authorship of the Pentateuch is contravened and his narrative is represented as being unhistorical and involving contradictions and impossibilities.

beginning with the very first step of it—*the Descent into Egypt.*" (Chap. II. § 18, p. 17.)

Believing that many of the difficulties stated by the Bishop are new to the public mind of *protestant* England, though not quite so new in *neological* Germany; and knowing that some time must elapse before a work, entitled to be considered a full answer to all the Bishop's objections, can be submitted to the public; the writer has deemed that he should be doing a service to the cause of truth, by at once publishing what he humbly hopes is a searching Analysis of the facts of the life of Jacob and his Sons, which have a bearing directly or indirectly on the question of "THE DESCENT INTO EGYPT." If it can be shewn, that the Bishop's criticism on this point is at fault; if it can be rendered probable, that, in his anxiety to search out difficulties *but not to remove them,* or to raise doubts *but not to allay them,* he has overlooked the necessity he was under to examine the Hebrew and Greek originals, and has solely depended on a translation, which (valuable as it may be) is certainly not infallible, while he seems to have accepted the marginal chronology of the English version as an acknowledged portion of the Mosaic statements; the Christian world may feel reassured, and calmly wait for that thorough answer, which the Bishop's attack is sure yet to elicit from the stores of sound scriptural erudition still remaining amongst us.

The writer, in contributing this his mite to the Christian treasury, has divided his work into two portions: in the former, he has particularly considered the Evangelist's narrative of the Infancy and Youth of our Lord Jesus Christ—Luke ii. 40—52; to which he has prefixed some general remarks on the sources of the Bishop's errors, and reasons for still believing the commonly received account of the Authorship of the Pentateuch: in the latter, he has considered the Descent of Jacob into Egypt.

W. J. SPRY.

Devonport, November 10th, 1862.

Extract from "the Devonport Independent" of Saturday, November 8, 1862.

PLYMOUTH INSTITUTION.—On Thursday, October 30th, a highly interesting lecture was delivered by Mr. W. J. Spry, at the Athenæum, on "The Evidences (Historical and Traditional, Linguistical, Geological, and Astronomical) of the Antiquity of the Existence of Man on the Earth." W. F. Moore, Esq., the President, was in the chair. The lecturer, in opening his subject, set forth the different views entertained as to the origin of man, and claimed to use the Jewish scriptures as a very ancient historical document. He next reviewed the early history and traditions of Egypt, Babylonia, India, and China; and subjected the statements of Plato, Herodotus, Diodorus, Manetho, Berosus, and others to a rigid analysis, shewing the untrustworthiness of the extravagant claims to a high antiquity contained in the traditions of the respective nations, and that the various reporters of these several accounts were at least a thousand years more recent than the writer of the Jewish account. The reasons assigned by Bunsen for his opinion—that the creation of Adam took place fully 20,000 years ago, as evidenced by the time necessary for the formation of various languages, were shewn to be without sufficient foundation; and next the lecturer examined the hypothesis of the anonymous author of "The Genesis of the Earth and of Man"—that the Bible indicated two creations of men, the former of which was the negro race; and shewed that the criticism of the Hebrew text, on which the author relied, was a fallacy. Referring to the assumptions of Geologists, the lecturer remarked that many geologists (including in the number some men of acknowledged high scientific attainments) lay claim to immense periods or ages, amounting in some instances to millions of years, for the deposition and consolidation of the strata of the earth's crust; while they admit that it is only in the latest deposits, that any remains of man or of his industry are to be found; but even for the latter they claim an antiquity, which they estimate by tens of thousands of years He contended that those immense periods rest on a very different basis scientifically regarded from that on which the speculations of the astronomer are erected—the immense distances in space and tens of thousands of years in time spoken of by the astronomer are well-reasoned inferences drawn from 4,000 years of observations, and confirmed in modern days by the exact recurrence of the phenomena of the heavens at the predicted times; while the more extended periods of geologists are mere hypotheses to explain the present appearances of the earth, but not proved facts; Geology itself being, as it were, a science only of yesterday, whose observations scarcely extend over a century. The lecturer proved how baseless was Mr. Leonard Horner's assumption of an antiquity for man in Egypt of 13,500 years, which he estimated from the circumstance of a piece of pottery having been taken up from a depth of 39 feet in a boring in the sediment of the Nile at Memphis, supposing it to have been deposited at the rate of three and a half inches in a century; but, as fragments of burnt brick were brought up from the very bottom of the same boring, and the use of burnt brick was only introduced into Egypt by the Romans, the actual antiquity was thus clearly less than 2,000 years. The lecturer next pointed out that all the existing languages of the earth have been developed according to three primary forms of thought; and showed that the long periods of time required by the anti-scripturists for their deverelopment were not warranted by the known facts, while the latter ignore the statement of the confusion of tongues at Babel. Referring to Chronology, the lecturer showed that the true date, deducible from the Scriptures as that of the Deluge, is about 3155 B.C. He examined the monumental evidence furnished by the Egyptian temples and tombs, and by the bricks and cylinders taken from the mounds of Southern Chaldæa, and their respective explanations by Mr. R. S. Poole and General Sir H. C. Rawlinson, corroborated by astronomical calculations. He proved that the extravagant periods of the Hindus and Cingalese were mere astronomical myths or numerical calculations, having no historical significance whatever. Lastly, he adduced the true dates of the earliest astronomical observations by the Chaldæans, Indians, and Chinese: the Indians commencing their Cali Yug, from which their present computation of years is dated, at the year 3102 B.C., at which time they record an observation of the sun's and moon's longitude; and the Chinese observations giving the particulars of an eclipse of the sun in 2155 B.C.; both of which have been verified by means of our modern astronomical knowledge. The lecturer concluded thus:—"I have shown that the earliest proved chronologial records of the Egyptians, Chaldæans, Indians, and Chinese are of the respective dates of 2717, 2234, 3102, and 2357 (or, perhaps, 2952) B.C.; and I have also shewn that the true scriptural date of the Deluge is 3155 B.C., if not about a century still earlier. I, therefore, confidently assert that the true dates of the earliest astronomical observations and the ascertained facts of the early histories of Egypt, Assyria and Babylon, India, and China, as testified by existing monumental and other remains, are in no way inconsistent with sound criticism of the scriptural date of the Deluge, and are quite reconcileable with the Hebrew history." The reading of the paper was listened to throughout with the deepest attention, by a very numerous auditory of the members and their friends; and was followed by a very animated discussion, in which the

Revs. E. Risk and Tracey, and Messrs. Bartlett, Bate (F.R.S.), Weymouth, Shelley, Balkwill, and others took part, and which was only ended by the arrival of the hour for closing. We have been informed that our townsman Mr. Spry intends to use a portion of the contents of his lecture for a work he is about to prepare against the views of Bishop Colenso, Von Bohlen, and others, to be entitled "Moses, not Samuel, the writer of the Pentateuch. Genesis a history, not a fiction."

Chapter I.

St. Luke's statement concerning the Infancy of Our Lord considered, with particular reference to the question—"Was the knowledge of the Lord Jesus Christ limited? and did or could He know more than any other pious and learned Jew of the age in which He lived, as to the Authorship of the Pentateuch?" preceded by remarks on the sources of Bishop Colenso's errors, and some reasons for still believing the Pentateuch to be the work of Moses.

"HAD ye believed Moses, ye would have believed Me ; for he wrote of Me : but, if ye believe not his writings, how shall ye believe My words ?" (John v. 46 & 47.) These words of our Lord imply (amongst other things) His conviction (1) that Moses was acquainted with the art of writing, and that he practised the art ; (2) that the writings of Moses (*i.e.*, the particulars of what he committed to writing) had been preserved till our Lord's day, and were known to the Jews of that age ; and (3) that those writings did contain prophecies applicable to Himself. The so called criticism of German rationalists has denied or doubted concerning all these points; and Bishop Colenso, having drunk deeply at that poisoned fountain, and thereby lost the right use of his reasoning faculties, has offered incense on the altar of his idol. Bewildered by the smoke he has himself produced, the light that was in him has become darkness,* and he has fancied that he has a call to become a missionary from the land of the intelligent Zulu Kaffirs to enlighten the poor ignorant deluded people of protestant England. The bishop, it

---

* Matt. vi. 23.

seems, thinks that a man may be a Christian, even if he deny that Moses ever wrote a book; although the plain consequence of such an hypothesis must be, that Jesus Christ was Himself either deceived or a deceiver: the former consequence is adopted by the bishop. If, then, our Lord were *deceived*, how, we would ask, can Christianity be a revelation from God? or in what respect does it differ from Mohammedism? The bishop, too, considers that himself, born more than eighteen centuries since our Lord, and thirty-four centuries since the assumed time of Moses; born, too, in England, a country where the manners and customs of the people are continually varying, whilst in the East, the country of Moses and Jesus, manners and customs change not from generation to generation and from century to century— the bishop, I say, considers that he knows better than Christ; and believes that German criticism of the language used (aided with the application of Colenso's arithmetic to the numbers found) in the collection of books called the Pentateuch, can prove to a demonstration that Moses was not their author, and that their contents are not matters of fact. Here let it be remembered, that our Lord was born a Jew, in the very land which His nation had then occupied (with only a brief interval of 70 years) during a period of sixteen centuries from the time when Moses led their ancestors to its conquest, and amongst a people who still spoke a dialect of the language in which the books were written, and who religiously regarded Moses as their great lawgiver, while they jealously adhered (as they still do as far as their being exiles permits) to the peculiar form of worship and customs which he was believed to have introduced and established, and their observance of which led to the enmity of their neighbours and repeated persecutions; and, when these things have been well considered, let any reasoning being say whether the bishop and his German friends, on the one hand, or the Lord Jesus Christ and the Jewish people, on the other, are likely to be the best judges of the matter of fact as to the authorship of those writings. It is, then, because as an individual I conceive that the religion professed by the great mass of the people of England (a religion, be it remembered, on the universal diffusion of whose teachings the happiness of the human race is believed to depend) must be overthrown, if the bishop's hypothesis can be established, and because I humbly hope myself to be doing battle in the cause of truth against error, that I have undertaken to expose some, at least, of his fallacies.

As I intend to analyze the bishop's statements, as well as the words of Scripture which I shall oppose to his views; and as many of my readers may not have the bishop's book by their side, when they are reading this; I shall occasionally quote passages at length from his work.

In the first 9 pages of his "Preface," the bishop enlists the sympathy of his readers, by the manner in which he submits the doubts and difficulties, whereby his mind had begun to be agitated, for the friendly advice of a Professor of Divinity; but the letter he had written he did not send; and he subsequently sought assistance from a source, which he must needs have expected to add to his scepticism rather than to remove difficulties. It would seem, by his own statements and by the results he has arrived at, as if German commentators and critics were the great objects of his study, rather than the plain unvarnished statements of the Hebrew and Greek originals. As a consequence of this course, he says "I did not now need counsel or assistance to relieve my own personal doubts: in fact, I had no longer any doubts—my former misgivings had been changed to certainties:" so he decided that the letter he had written, but which he had detained for a time to see what effect further study and consideration would have upon his views, he would not forward at all. "*Facilis descensus Averni:*"* rapid, indeed, was his downward progress in error. He speedily resolved to set about converting the world to his new reading of the Biblical record, and to seek to convince the whole Church "of the unhistorical character of very considerable portions of the Mosaic narrative." He says "I use the expression *unhistorical* or *not historically true* rather than *fictitious*, since the word *fiction* is frequently understood to imply a conscious dishonesty on the part of the writer—*an intention to deceive.* Yet, in writing the story of the Exodus from the ancient legends of his people, the Scripture writer may have had no more consciousness of doing wrong or of practising historical deception than Homer had or any of the early Roman annalists." ("Preface," p. xvii.) We here see the estimated value in the bishop's eyes of the earliest portion of the Divine Revelation : that, which we have been taught to believe as the narrative of a very important event in the history of God's chosen people, recorded at the time of its occurrence by Moses and Joshua, the respective leaders of that people out of Egyptian bondage and into the Promised Land, is here compared with the tale of the Trojan War formed into a poem by Homer, a man concerning whose age and birth-place the learned world

---

* Virgil.

are in doubt, but who certainly lived some centuries after (and has never been supposed to be contemporary with) the event he has celebrated; or the account of the early Roman kings, between whom and the writers of the narrations we have not less than four or five centuries must have elapsed. Yet, in justice to the bishop, we should consider that he seems to have adopted the views of De Wette and other Germans—that the books attributed to Moses and Joshua could not have been written at the times of the events themselves mentioned in them; while some of these critics, at least, regard Samuel, or some writer of his time, as the author or compiler of the Pentateuch and Joshua. Let, then, the reader turn to the 12th chapter of the 1st book of Samuel, and read the prophet's narration to the assembly of the people of Israel on his resigning his Judgeship: let him consider the highly moral tone of Samuel's address, his claim to honesty of conduct and uprightness of purpose, and his appeal to the people for his truthfulness; and surely the reader will say, if his mind be not already warped by scepticism, this man certainly could not have forged the so called Mosaic narrative and then palmed it off upon the people as a true account. I have purposely used the word *forged* here; for, if the Mosaic books be "not historically true," they constitute one of the vilest forgeries and impostures, of which any portion of the human race has ever been the dupes or the victims.

The bishop, having " arrived at the certainty that the account of the Exodus, whatever value it may have, is *not historically true*," does not submit the result of his labors to the Professor of Divinity, to whom he had originally intended to send his letter asking for "advice and assistance, such as" (he says) "few are better able to give than yourself;" but he submits his work, before deciding to publish it, to a friend; at least, the bishop calls him so. Judging from the advice he gave, I deem the bishop's "friend" one of the enemies of man's moral welfare. The bishop says " He thought then (though now approving fully of the course which I am taking) that such an open declaration of the sum and substance of my work ' might tend to prejudice the reader, and probably make him more inclined to become hardened against the force of the arguments;' and he suggested that I might do more wisely to conceal, as it were, my purpose for a time, and lead the reader gradually on, till he ' would arrive of himself, almost unawares,' at the same conclusions as my own." ("Preface," p. xix.) The bishop is, it seems, the more honest of the two; but, having so far made a clean breast of it, he ought to have completed his confession, and let the world know the name of his confidant—that we may be the better able to judge of the value of his advice: in such a case, *the writer's hue does concern the town.*

In pp. xxi.—xxiii., the bishop propounds six reasons why, in his opinion, " the phenomena in the Pentateuch, which show so decisively its unhistorical character, have not yet, as far as" he is " aware, been set forth before the eyes of English readers." His first proposition is, that " some of these difficulties would only be likely to occur to one in the same position as" himself, " engaged as a Missionary in translating the Scriptures ;" and assumes that, " in a practical point of view," he has regarded them " in a way in which an English student would scarcely think of looking at them." He tells us (p. vi.) that he has "translated the New Testament completely, and several parts of the Old, among the rest the books of Genesis and Exodus, into the Zulu tongue." The bishop surely overlooks the fact, that within the present century numerous translations of the Scriptures into languages in which they did not previously exist, and revisions of the translations (and even new ones) in the languages of peoples professing Christianity, have been made, chiefly by learned men speaking the English language; and have been printed and disseminated by the agency of " the British and Foreign Bible Society" and "the Society for promoting Christian Knowledge." But, whatever may be the bishop's other qualifications for the task of translating the Scriptures, there is one, I fear, which he has overlooked. From the manner in which he has propounded his various objections, I should estimate that he has translated the Scriptures into Zulu, not out of the original Greek and Hebrew, but out of the English; and that, too, not the plain and simple meaning of the English as it appears to an ordinary reader, but with the addition of notes and commentaries, which (however valuable they may be in some instances) must be diligently guarded against in the mind of a translator, lest he should accept them as a part of the Sacred Text. Into this error I shall hereafter prove the bishop to have fallen. And, assuredly, after what has emanated from his pen, neither of the before mentioned societies nor any of the missionary societies will adopt the bishop's Translation without a searching revision, which must be as laborious as the making of a new translation: so that his labors in this direction must have become nearly worthless.

His second proposition is, that "such studies as these" (*i.e.*, the phenomena in the Pentateuch to which he has before referred) "have made very little progress as yet among the clergy and laity of *England;* and so the English mind, with its practical common-sense, has scarcely yet been brought to bear upon them." By his Italicising the word '*England,*' I infer him to imply that in some other countries (*Germany,* for instance) such studies are very prevalent—a fact, with which many of us are but too well acquainted ; and I trust it will be long, very long, ere the practical English mind will run riot in the race after the illogical mysticism of tobacco-smoke-beclouded, beer-bemuddled German professors, who fancy that their microscopic eyes enable them to see farther into a millstone than other men can. If difficulties do start up in the way of any anxious inquirer in our still favored, God-fearing land, and he cannot find how to resolve them ; such an one will, I trust, make them known in some way, so that the minds of others may be turned to the consideration ; and, I doubt not, a proper solution will be found : but it is a very different thing, for a man to be seeking whether he cannot find out a difficulty ; and, when he fancies he has found one, endeavouring by quibbles to distract the attention of others in their attempts to unloose the knot.

The bishop's third proposition affecting the historical character of the Pentateuch is assuredly not new, as he himself admits : it is the old story of the difficulties attending the accounts of " the Creation, the Fall, and the Deluge ;" but, as he does not state them, confining his attention to " questioning the general historical truth of the story of the Exodus," it is not necessary for me here to make any further remark.

His fourth point is, "that English books upon the historical credibility of the Mosaic narrative are at present very few;" and that some, "which are written in defence of the ordinary view, pass by entirely the main points of difficulty, as if they were wholly unknown to the writers." It will not be able to be said in future, however, that we have no English book upon the historical *incredibility* of the Mosaic narrative; Bishop Colenso having done his best to supply the deficiency, if such there were.

The fifth article, having reference particularly to English translations of "the works of the so called orthodox German writers," whose commentaries, whilst exhibiting a mass of erudition, often bewilder the reader, claims no remarks from me in reply; as my observations will have reference solely to the words of the inspired writers, without troubling myself to defend commentators, however judicious their expositions may be presumed to be.

His sixth and last proposition is, that "writers of the liberal school in Germany take so completely for granted (either on mere critical grounds, or because they assume from the first the utter impossibility of miracles or supernatural revelations) the unhistorical character and non-Mosaic origin of the greater portion at least, if not the whole of the Pentateuch, that they do not generally take the trouble to test the credibility of the story, by entering into such matter-of-fact inquiries as are here made the basis of the whole argument." To the truth of the former portion of the bishop's remarks I am ready to bear testimony as far as my own reading has extended; but to the latter part I am not able to assent so readily. In regard to testing the credibility of the story, by examining the statistics contained in the Pentateuch (which is what I presume the bishop to mean by 'such matter-of-fact inquiries'), the germs of many of his investigations are to be found in the work of Von Bohlen, published at Königsberg in 1835. It is a singular circumstance, that the work to which I have now referred should have been published in England, for the first time, simultaneously with the bishop's production; and by the same publishers, too, Messrs. Longman and Co. The English edition is entitled "Historical and Critical Illustrations of the First Part of Genesis, from the German of Professor Von Bohlen, edited by James Heywood, M.A., F.R.S." The first remark I would here make is, that the translator is not mentioned, only the editor: the second, that the original work is " Genesis historico-critically illustrated ;" while the English edition extends only to the general " Introduc-

tion," vol. i., and the "Cosmogonies and Primæval History," vol. ii.
—the latter extending only as far as the 11th chapter of Genesis. The 1st volume (amongst other things) contains a general criticism of the Pentateuch, in which almost every conceivable difficulty, that the laborious researches of an untiring, plodding, enthusiastic German professor could find in the writings of others or himself invent, has been piled up into one huge heap: let the reader only fancy the "Introduction" to a book extending over 322 pages in 8vo. closely printed, about one-half of which, too, consists of notes in smaller type. Here we have questions submitted on the early records of the Hebrews, the invention of writing, the Mosaic authorship of the Pentateuch, the style of the language used, the connexion of the Israelites with Egypt, the geography of the East, the wanderings in the Desert, numerical inventions and exaggerations, statistical errors, inconsistencies and interpolations in the Pentateuch, the constitutional government of the Israelites, the Levitical system and hierarchy, &c., &c. Some of these questions are decided thus:— Writing, it is asserted, was unknown in the time of Moses and long afterwards; and, therefore, Moses could not have written the Pentateuch: the style of the writings is nearly 1000 years more recent than the generally assumed age of their composition: Samuel, or some writer of his day, was the first compiler of the account of the Exodus;

and the Pentateuch itself was not completed till long after the establishment of the kingdoms of Judah and Israel: the early Israelitish connexion with Egypt is denied, on the assumed ground—that the manners and customs attributed in the Pentateuch to the Egyptians did not exist in Egypt till centuries after the supposed dates of Abraham, Joseph, or even Moses: and, lastly, the geography of the books is declared frequently to be mistaken and erroneous. The work of Von Bohlen, it should be remembered, was published 27 years ago, and the author has been dead more than 22 years: the researches of Botta, Layard, Rawlinson, Taylor, Loftus, and others in the East, have since established it as a fact—that writing was used, at least in Chaldæa, the birth-place of Abraham, centuries before the time of Moses; while new light has been thrown, by the labors of these and other learned men, on the ancient geography of the East, disproving much that is contained in Von Bohlen: nevertheless, the English editor, who has introduced here and there long notes of his own (there is one in the 2d volume extending over 17 pages), pretending to supply information from the most recent scientific discoveries and researches, has not once hinted at any thing which has occurred since Von Bohlen's day to call his statements and criticisms in question or to disprove them. Is such a course as this, I would ask, honest? I would further remark, that Von Bohlen's work was dedicated to his friends Gesenius and De Wette, and with the writings of the latter the bishop admits his acquaintance, but he no where even mentions Von Bohlen. It would be a singular episode to all this, if it should hereafter be found, that Bishop Colenso had been the translator of Von Bohlen's book, and that its editor (Mr. James Heywood) was the friend of whom the bishop speaks in his own "Preface." Let me here, however, guard against misapprehension: I have no other ground for these suppositions than the coincidence of publication, to which I have before referred, and a certain adaptation of matter and arrangement, which seems to pervade the both works and to make one almost a sequel to the other. The bishop, however, may be called upon to say—whether he had not some cognisance of the intended publication of the translation of Von Bohlen on Genesis, before its appearance was announced?

We come now to the more immediate subject of this chapter. At p. xxix. of his "Preface," the bishop says "I shall not shrink from the duty of examining on behalf of others into the question, in what way the Interpretation of the New Testament is affected by the unhistorical character of the Pentateuch;" though he adds "I would gladly leave to other hands the above inquiry at greater length for the general reader." He proceeds, however, to say "There may be some, who will say that such words as those in John vi. 46, 47—'For, had ye believed Moses, ye would have believed Me, for *he wrote* of Me; but, if ye believe not his writings, how shall ye believe my words?' or in Luke xx. 37—'Now, that the dead are raised, even *Moses shewed* at the bush' [*i.e.*, in the passage about 'the bush'], 'when he called* the LORD the God of Abraham and the God of Isaac and the God of Jacob;' or in Luke xvi. 29—'*They have Moses* and the Prophets; let them hear them;' and *v.* 31 —'*If they hear not Moses* and the Prophets, neither will they be persuaded, though one rose from the dead;'—are, at once, decisive upon the point of Moses' authorship of the Pentateuch; since they imply that our Lord Himself believed in it; and, con-

---

* "Calleth" in our authorised version, as it is in the Greek. The variation is the bishop's, but is of no consequence one way or another (as far as I am aware) in this argument; and I have only remarked it, lest it might be attributed to myself.

sequently, to assert that Moses did *not* write these books, would be to contradict the words of Christ and to impugn His veracity." ("Preface," pp. xxix. & xxx.) The bishop adds that "to make use of such an argument is, indeed, to make belief in Christianity itself depend entirely upon the question—whether Moses wrote the Pentateuch, or not." He endeavours to destroy the force of this objection from three considerations; the first of which is, "that such words can only be supposed to apply to *certain parts* of the Pentateuch;" and that "it would become, even thus, a question for a reverent criticism—to determine what passages give signs of *not* having been written by Moses." (P. xxx.) His second objection is, "that, in making use of such expressions, our Lord did but accommodate His words to the current popular language of the day." (P. xxxi.) To these reasons I need not stay to reply, as it is evident that the bishop himself depends principally upon his third point, which I shall proceed to quote in full :—

"Lastly, it is perfectly consistent with the most entire and sincere belief in our Lord's Divinity, to hold, as many do, that, when He vouchsafed to become a 'Son of Man,' He took our nature fully, and voluntarily entered into all the conditions of humanity, and (amongst others) into that which makes our growth in all ordinary knowledge *gradual* and *limited*. We are expressly told, in Luke ii. 52, that 'Jesus increased in *wisdom*' as well as in '*stature*.' It is not supposed, that, in His human nature, He was acquainted, more than any educated Jew of the age, with the mysteries of all modern sciences; nor, with St. Luke's expressions before us, can it be seriously maintained, that, as an *infant* or *young child*, He possessed a knowledge surpassing that of the most pious and learned adults of His nation upon the subject of the authorship and age of the different portions of the Pentateuch. At what period, then, of His life upon earth is it to be supposed that He had granted to Him as the Son of Man, *supernaturally*, full and accurate information on these points, so that He should be expected to speak about the Pentateuch in other terms than any other devout Jew of that day would have employed? Why should it be thought, that He would speak with certain *Divine* knowledge on this matter, more than upon other matters of ordinary science or history?" ("Preface," pp. xxxi. & xxxii.)

This passage contains, as I believe, a series of errors, which I humbly hope to be able to expose, and (God giving me His grace) to confute by a rigorous analysis of the original words of the inspired writers. The Bishop talks of our Lord's Divinity, not

His Deity ; and it is evident from other portions of the paragraph
I have quoted, that he does not believe in the Godhead [Θεότης,
Theotés *] of the Lord Jesus Christ. As I am writing for the
benefit of persons who are not skilled in the learned languages,
as well as for those who are ; I shall here enter into explanations,
which may appear superfluous to some. Many are apt to suppose
that there is no difference in meaning between the words 'Divinity' and 'Deity' : nevertheless, the difference is very considerable. The words are Latin : 'Deity,' from the Latin *Deus* (a

---

* It becomes necessary here to explain that throughout these remarks, wherever I
have considered it to be necessary to quote words or sentences from the learned
languages, which are generally written in characters different from those in common
use with us, I have accompanied them with a representation of the sounds in our
letters, together with a translation. If I have quoted a word or phrase only, I have
inclosed its representative in brackets after it: thus "[*Theotés*]." But, when I have
quoted a whole verse or more, I have given the whole in Greek or Hebrew characters,
with the representative sounds immediately below. I have repeated these representative sounds ; but occasionally, when the English translation seemed to require it, with
a slightly different arrangement of the words : and, above each of the Greek or Hebrew
words so represented, I have put the English translation ; while, whenever more than
one English word seemed to be required to give the sense of the original, I have joined
such words together with hyphens ; thus "This-was-happening." I have done this for
the benefit of the mere English reader, to enable him to follow my argument as far as
possible. I would also here remark that I have not generally referred to the classic
writers for my illustrations of the Greek ; because I have considered that the Greek of
the Septuagint and of the New Testament, being what is called Hellenistic Greek, differs
considerably in its style, and frequently in its usage of words, from Classical Greek.
The writers of the Septuagint and the New Testament were Jews, to whom Greek was
not a native (but an acquired) language ; and the influence of Jewish ideas and Hebrew
phraseology is, consequently, every where apparent in those writings.

god), is properly represented by our Saxon word *Godhead* 'Divinity,' from the Latin *Divinus* (the quality of a *Divus* *— i.e.*, a godlike one, a deified man), means *Godlikeness* or *Godship*. These words in Greek (at least, in the Greek of the Sacred Scriptures) are Θεότης [*Theotés*], Deity (from θεὸς [*theos*], a god), and Θειότης [*Theiotés*], Divinity (from θεῖος [*theios*], godlike, divine), respectively. The latter word is used by St. Paul, when arguing concerning the revelations (as they may be called) of natural religion : he says " Because that, which may be known of God, is manifest in them; for God hath shewed it unto them. For the invisible things of Him from the creation of the world are clearly seen, being understood by the things that are made, even His eternal power and Godhead [*Theiotés*, Divinity, Godlikeness]." (Rom. i. 19 & 20.) But, when he is arguing about the revelations of spiritual religion (on a matter, which is—not in itself unreasonable, but beyond or above our reasoning powers), Paul says " Beware! lest any man spoil you through philosophy and vain deceit, after the tradition of men, after the rudiments of the world, and not after Christ; for in Him dwelleth all the fulness of the Godhead [*Theotés*, Deity] bodily."

---

* *Divus* was an epithet frequently applied by the Romans to their emperors and others: thus, Julius Cæsar was called " Divus Julius" (*i.e.*, the divine Julius).

(Col. ii. 8 & 9.) Further argument on this point I deem unnecessary.

The next phrase of the bishop's to be noted is his insidious introduction of the indefinite article, instead of the definite one, before the words 'Son of Man.' The bishop, it will be seen, says "when He" [our Lord] "vouchsafed to become a 'Son of Man':" it is true, he does not pretend to quote the "a" as a part of our Lord's title — his punctuation shows that ; but such things are frequently overlooked in reading a book rapidly : on the other hand, the epithet of the Lord Jesus Christ in the New Testament is always "the Son of Man ;" the Greek constantly using the article ὁ [*ho*], answering to our English "the," as a prefix. This, taken in connexion with what follows, clearly shews the bishop's Socinianism.

We next come to the assertion, that our Lord's "growth in all ordinary knowledge" was "*gradual* and *limited*." That our Lord was born an infant, after the usual period of gestation ; that His mother nursed Him, as other infants are nursed ; that He acquired speech &c., as other children do ; and that He increased in height and bulk from childhood, through youth, and until He reached manhood, as other persons do—are all of them,

I presume, matters about which no doubt needs to exist. I do not believe that He spoke as soon as He was born; but I must take exception to the assertion, that there was any *limit* to His knowledge: His knowledge might (and, probably, did) unfold itself, without any effort humanly speaking. The Volume of Inspiration no where tells of His going to school, or of His having a tutor; and the fables on this head, in "the Gospel of the Infancy" and other spurious works, are unworthy of consideration. But the Scriptures do not leave us in doubt on this head: the Jews are our witnesses, when they said "How knoweth This Man letters, having never learned?" (John vii. 15.) And here I must warn the reader to discriminate between 'knowledge' and 'wisdom.' The bishop speaks of them, in the passage I am now criticising, as if they were synonymous; but they are not so. These terms in Greek are γνῶσις [*gnôsis*] and σοφία [*sophia*], corresponding to the Latin words *scientia* and *sapientia* respectively; the former meaning *science* (or *knowledge* acquired by the use of the bodily senses), and the latter *wisdom* (or *wit's doom* —meaning the judgement [*doom*] given by the mind, after a thorough consideration of the acquired knowledge [*wit*] submitted to it): in other words, 'science' or 'knowledge' is a sensible [sensational] process, and 'wisdom' is a purely mental one. In the passages in the 2d chapter of Luke, the evangelist each time uses the word σοφία [*sophia*],' wisdom.' The passages stand thus in our English version:—"And the Child grew, and waxed strong in spirit, filled with wisdom ; and the grace of God was upon Him " (*v*. 40). " And Jesus increased in wisdom and stature, and in favor with God and man" (*v*. 52). The words ' grew ' and ' increased ' are generally taken to be synonymous in English ; but the word rendered ' increased ' in the latter verse is a very different one, in the Greek original, from that which is rendered ' grew ' in the former verse, and of very different meaning. As the bishop has drawn a conclusion from the evangelist's words in the 52d verse, which, however it may appear to be warranted by the English translation, does not seem to be supportable from the words of the original ; I shall analyze the both verses, giving the Greek, accompanied by a translation of each word :—

V. 40. Τὸ δὲ παιδίον ηὔξανε, καὶ ἐκραταιοῦτο πνεύματι,
         To de paidion éuxane, kai ekrataiouto pneumati,
πληρούμενον σοφίας· καὶ χάρις Θεοῦ ἦν ἐπ' αὐτό.
pléroumenon sophias : kai charis Theou én ep' auto.

But the   Child   grew,   and   was - becoming - powerful
De   to   paidion   éuxane, kai   ekrataiouto
in-spirit,   being-full   of-wisdom ; and the-grace of-God was
pneumati, pléroumenon sophias :   kai charis Theou én
upon Him.
ep' auto.

Here we find that, as our Lord grew up, His intellectual [spiritual] power developed itself: He was full of wisdom (*i.e.*, He did *not* get wisdom *gradually*; it was already in Him; or, as St. Paul says, the fulness [πλήρωμα, *plêrôma*] of the Godhead was in Him bodily): and every grace, whether of body or mind, was shewing itself in Him.

It will be seen, that I have rendered *ep' auto* by "upon Him," as the authorised version reads: literally, however, the phrase is "upon It" (*i.e.*, the Child); because the pronoun *auto* is in the neuter gender in the Greek, agreeing with *to paidion* (the Child), which is of the neuter gender.

V. 52. Καὶ Ἰησοῦς προέκοπτε σοφίᾳ, καὶ ἡλικίᾳ, καὶ
    Kai Iêsous proekopte sophiai, kai hêlikiai, kai
χάριτι παρὰ Θεῷ καὶ ἀνθρώποις.
chariti para Theôi kai anthrôpois.

And Jesus was-preceding in-wisdom, and in-appearance, and
Kai Iêsous   proekopte   sophiai, kai   hêlikiai, kai
in-grace before God and   men.
chariti para Theôi kai anthrôpois.

Hence it appears, that Jesus naturally took precedence of other men in wisdom and in nobleness of countenance; while

God's favor was so apparent in Him, that all who knew Him acknowledged Him as being something superior to themselves.

As to the exact meaning of *proekopte*, which I have here rendered "was preceding," instead of "increased" (as it is in our common translation), I would remark that the root is προκόπτω [*prokoptô*], being a word compounded of πρὸ [*pro*] and κόπτω [*koptô*]. The meaning of the preposition *pro* is invariably 'before,' whether in time or in place: it is sometimes, however, rendered 'forth' (as coming forth from something), which (it is apparent) still retains the idea of *before:* in the instance under consideration, it means 'beforehand.' The verb *koptô* means 'I chop or cut off,' or (as applied to the coining of money) 'I cut out.' Hence, *prokoptô* means 'I am beforehand cutting out,' 'I from the first take precedence,' 'I excel.' Thus Jesus, as a child, *excelled* his fellow-mortals from the beginning: He did *not increase* or grow up *gradually* to a position of being respected : His appearance and the wisdom of His sayings at once claimed men's respect and attention.

My rendering of *hêlikiai* by "in appearance," instead of "stature" (as in our authorised version), comes next to be considered. The Greek root of this word is Ἥλιος [*hêlios*], 'the

Sun': this Plato considers to be derived from ἅλς [*hals*], 'the sea'; because, as soon as the Sun seems to rise out of the sea, men rise and proceed about their daily avocations. Others have deduced it from 'salt,' which is another meaning of *hals*; because, as salt is a preserver, so the Sun preserves and nourishes things. It has always appeared to me, that *Hêlios*, the Greek name for 'the Sun-god,' had its origin from the Hebrew אל [*Al* or *El*] and Arabic *Allah*, commonly rendered 'GOD'; but of which the true meaning appears to be 'Greatness,' 'Strength,' and 'Intelligence'; and this, because (as we know) the worship of the Sun was the earliest form of idolatry—mankind having regarded that body, from the numerous benefits they derived from its light and heat, as a visible symbol of *the Supreme Intelligence*. From Ἥλιος [*hêlios*], 'the Sun,' comes the adjective ἡλίκος [*hêlikos*], 'sunny'; commonly used in the senses of 'as great as,' 'as old as,' 'very strong,' or 'mighty.' Again, from this adjective ἡλίκος [*hêlikos*] comes the substantive ἡλικία [*hêlikia*], which should properly imply 'sunniness'; but of which the meanings, as used by the classical writers, appear to be 'old age,' 'maturity,' 'being of full age,' 'the state of manhood,' and 'stature' (in the sense of 'full growth'). It is in the last named sense of *full height*, that our Lord used the word *hêlikia*, when he said "Which of you by taking thought can add one cubit unto his stature?" (Matt.

vi. 27.) Again, when our Lord had given sight to the "man who was blind from his birth," and the Pharisees questioned his parents concerning the manner in which he had obtained his sight, they said "He is of age: ask him!" (John ix. 21 & 23.) The words in the original are "αὐτὸς ἡλικίαν ἔχει" [*autos hêlikian echei*], which is literally "himself full-growth hath" (*i.e.*, he has attained his full-growth, or is of mature age to be capable of answering for himself). Lastly, St. Paul, speaking of Sarah's faith, says that she "was delivered of a child, when she was past age." (Heb. xi. 11.) The Greek is "παρὰ καιρὸν ἡλικίας ἔτεκεν" [*para kairon hêlikias eteken*], properly "at the-time of-mature-age she-bare." It is clear, then, that *hêlikia* does not mean 'stature' in a growing or increasing sense: it only means 'full stature.' From all that I have said, I infer the proper sense of *hêlikia* to be 'a sunniness of countenance,' 'true nobility,' 'a general comeliness of face and figure, combined with gracefulness of manner,' 'mature appearance.' And, hence, the inaccuracy of our received version is shewn; for, if the word rendered "stature" can only mean (as I have shewn it to mean) *full growth*, this cannot be the subject of any *increase*. The bishop's construction of Luke ii. 52 is thus evidently erroneous.

I have rendered *para* "before," rather than "with." Its strict sense, when followed by a dative (as is the case in the passage I am analyzing), being 'in regard to,' 'in comparison with,' or 'alongside of.' The sense of the passage is, correctly, that Jesus was in favor both with regard to God and men.

Lastly, the bishop's assertion, that St. Luke's expressions shew that Jesus did not possess " a knowledge surpassing that of the most pious and learned adults of His nation," and that it is not to be expected that He should "speak about the Pentateuch in other terms than any other devout Jew of that day would have employed," requires to be considered; and here we must analyze St. Luke's statement concerning Christ's disputation, at "twelve years old," with the doctors in the Temple. "And it came to pass, that, after three days, they found Him in the temple, sitting in the midst of the doctors, both hearing them and asking them questions. And all that heard Him were astonished at His understanding and answers." (Luke ii. 46 & 47.) That the words I have just quoted support the bishop's assertion I undoubtingly deny; whilst I affirm that the evangelist's own expressions, which I shall now proceed to analyze, lead to a directly contrary conclusion.

V. 46. Καὶ ἐγένετο, μεθ' ἡμέρας τρεῖς εὗρον αὐτὸν ἐν
Kai egeneto, meth' hêmeras treis heuron auton en

τῷ ἱερῷ καθεζόμενον ἐν μέσῳ τῶν διδασκάλων, καὶ
tôi hierôi kathezomenon en mesôi tôn didaskalôn, kai

ἀκούοντα αὐτῶν καὶ ἐπερωτῶντα αὐτούς. V. 47. Ἐξίσταντο
akouonta autôn kai eperôtônta autous. Existanto

δὲ πάντες οἱ ἀκούοντες αὐτοῦ, ἐπὶ τῇ συνέσει καὶ ταῖς
de pantes hoi akouontes autou, epi têi sunesei kai tais

ἀποκρίσεσιν αὐτοῦ.
apokrisesin autou.

And this-was-happening — after three days they-found
Kai egeneto, meth' treis hêmeras heuron

Him in the temple, being-seated in the-midst of-the
auton en tôi hierôi kathezomenon en mesôi tôn

teachers, both hearing from-them (*i.e.*, listening to them)
didascalôn, kai akouonta autôn

and interrogating them. But all those hearing
kai eperôtônta autous. De pantes hoi akouontes

from-Him (*i.e.*, who were listening to Him) were-exstaticised
autou existanto,

at the manner-of-bringing-things-together and the
epi têi sunesei kai tais

deductions-drawn by-Him.
apokrisesin autou.

Here we find that our Lord, when only twelve years of age, having allowed His relatives to quit Jerusalem without Him, had remained behind to test the knowledge of the most learned men (*the teachers*) of His nation. He takes His place among them; and, when His friends return to search for Him, they find Him seated amid these learned-ones, listening to their expositions and then amazing them by His questions upon their own statements. The Record states that they were bewildered, bewitched, or in an exstacy, at the way in which He grouped things together; and, when He had so arranged or classified the ideas, the inferences He drew were equally beyond the powers of the doctors to attain to—they were quite astounded. What limit, I would ask, does this statement put upon our Lord's knowledge, even in boyhood? and which of all the educated Jews of that age, or of the most pious and learned adults of His nation, is to be compared for his wisdom with this Most Wonderful Child? " Whence, then," we may well ask, as did the Jews of old, "hath This Man this wisdom?" (Matt. xiii. 54 & 56.)

It will be seen, that much of the translation I have here given of Luke ii. 46 & 47 is paraphrastic; many of the words in the Greek not admitting, as far as I am aware, of any strictly verbal English synonymes: and hence arose the difficulty, which was felt by the authors of our received version, of giving a readable rendering of the original. I have rendered the word διδάσκαλοι [*didaskaloi*] (gen. *didaskalón*) "teachers," rather than "doctors" or "learned men"; the term *teachers* being the proper meaning: it is true, that the teachers were supposed to be learned men; but it is also equally true, that men may be doctors or learned, without their being professed teachers.

The common rendering of *eperótónta* by "asking questions" is open to the grave objection, that it would seem to imply inquiry for the instruction of the questioner, though that might not be its only meaning; but there is no such doubt implied in the word *eperótónta*. This is the accusative form of the participle ἐπερωτῶν [*eperótón*], compounded of ἐπί [*epi*], 'upon,' and ἐρωτῶν [*erótón*], 'questioning.' The whole word, therefore, is "upon-questioning" or "inter-rogating"; implying that, after hearing from the learned men what they had to state, He put questions upon their own statements, whereby their ignorance and imperfect knowledge became manifest. Thus He draws attention to Himself, and begins to exhibit His own knowledge by combining things together, concerning the collocation of which they had no previous ideas.

Existanto I have rendered by " were exstaticised "; considering that even the phrase " were astonished " fails to give the full force of the original. It comes from the verb ἐξίστημι [*existêmi*]; itself a compound of ἐξ [*ex*], ' out of,' and ἵστημι [*histêmi*], ' I stand *or* place ' In the passive or middle voice (the form in which the verb occurs here) the verb means ' I am put out of myself,' ' I am beside myself,' ' I am fascinated,' ' I am bewitched,' ' I am utterly bewildered,' ' I am amazed,' ' I am quite confounded,' ' I am out of my usual state,' and even ' I am stung to madness.' It is not improbable, that the senses of *fascination*, *bewilderment*, and *enraging even to madness*, are all at once included in the word used by the evangelist: some, it is likely, might be put in a fury with the thought, that those who had previously looked up to them as men of learning and wisdom would now see how little knowledge they really possessed, while they might also be envious of the great abilities He had manifested ; others would be overwhelmed with what they had heard; whilst others again would be charmed with the sweet manners of the Speaker, and be led willing captives by His eloquence and the gracious words of wisdom that proceeded out of His mouth. " Never man spake like This Man." (John vii. 46.)

Sunesei is the dative form (governed by the preposition *epi*) of σύνεσις [*sunesis* or *synesis*], 'a combining' or 'union'; from the verb συνίημι [*suniêmi*], 'I bring together,' 'I put together,' or 'I send together': the latter is compounded of σύν [*sun*], 'together,' and ἵημι [*hiêmi*], 'I send or throw.' *Synesis*, then, implies 'a placing together,' whether for the purpose of contrast or comparison. I have, therefore, preferred in my translation to use the phrase "His manner of bringing things together," rather than "His understanding."

Apokrisesin is the dative plural form of ἀπόκρισις [*apokrisis*], implying 'severance,' 'separation,' 'a dividing,' 'deduction,' or 'a judging from the circumstances accompanying any thing submitted for an opinion.' *Apokrisis* is compounded of ἀπό [*apo*], 'from,' and κρίσις [*krisis*], 'judgement': it is derived from the compound verb ἀποκρίνω [*apokrino*], 'I part asunder,' 'I separate,' 'I distinguish.' Hence, the meaning of *apokrisesin* appears to be "discriminations," "separations," "decisions," "judgements," or "deductions from," rather than "answers" (as given in our authorised version), which certainly conveys a very imperfect idea of the force and import of the Greek original.

The meaning conveyed by the whole sentence is—that all who heard Him were lost in wonderment at the wisdom displayed in His combinations and discriminations of various matters, while the conclusions He drew therefrom and His judgements on the whole utterly overwhelmed them by their novelty and yet manifest truthfulness.

I have concluded my analysis of the Evangelist's words; and shall now bring my remarks on the bishop's "Preface" to a conclusion. In direct opposition to his views, I feel persuaded that, whether I argue *à posteriori* (that is, go backward) from the words of Jesus to prove the truthfulness of Moses's statements, or *à priori* (that is, come forward) from the predictions of Moses to prove that Jesus was the promised Messiah, the Christ, the Anointed of Jehovah [" THE LORD thy God will raise up unto thee a Prophet from the midst of thee, of thy brethren, like unto me: unto Him ye shall hearken" (Deut. xviii. 15)] —the faithfulness of the one and the historical accuracy of the other must alike stand or fall together. On the truthfulness of the Jewish record Christ founded His claim to be called ' THE SON OF GOD '—" Search the Scriptures; for in them ye think ye have eternal life, and they are they which testify of Me!" (John v. 39.) As the Jews of old had Moses and the Prophets, so we in modern days have the Gospels of the evangelists and the Epistles of the apostles of our Lord; and, on our belief in or rejection of these as an in-every-respect truthful Revelation from "*the Father of Lights*"—the Giver of "*every good and every perfect gift*" (James i. 17), must depend our claim to be called Christians. If the narrative of the Exodus of the Children of Israel from Egypt be "not historically true," then the rest of the Pentateuch is a falsehood—a vile imposture upon the credulity of mankind; and the Jewish and Christian religious systems are alike worthless, being founded on an impudent lie. If Judaism be founded in truth, then the truth of Christianity can be established thereby: if Judaism be not true, neither can Christianity be true. And, again, if the truth of Christianity can be established by any means whatever, the truthfulness of the writings of the Old Testament must be thereby confirmed, and (among them) the historical accuracy of the five books to which we have attached the name of "the Pentateuch," and the fact of their Mosaic authorship. "*If they hear not Moses and the Prophets, neither will they be persuaded, though One rose from the dead!*" (Luke xvi. 31.)

Chapter ii.

THE circumstances of THE DESCENT OF JACOB INTO EGYPT considered, with particular reference to the questions—"Were there more than the 70 persons named in Gen. xlvi. who assembled in Egypt at the time of Jacob's going down?" and "Was Judah only 42 years old at that time?" including remarks on the nature of society in the East, on the prevalence of a state of bondage or servitude from the earliest historical times, on the households of Abraham and Jacob, on God's Covenant with Abraham, and on the duration of Jacob's residence in Padan-Aram; and preceded by observations on the Inspiration of the Pentateuch: with proofs that Bishop Colenso has attributed to Moses himself the mistakes of Commentators and the errors of Chronologers.

"ALL Scripture is given by inspiration of GOD:" such are the words of St. Paul, when, addressing Timothy, he remarked that he had "known the Holy Scriptures from" the time of his being "a child." (2 Tim. iii. 16 & 15.) Of course, this commendation of the study can only apply to the books of the New Testament by implication, as they did not exist at that time. The Holy Scriptures here referred to are those of the Old Testament, every book of which is thus unequivocally asserted to be God-inspired [θεόπνευστος, *theopneustos*].

Bishop Colenso, in his 1st Chapter, entitled "Introductory Remarks," says (p. 3) "The first five books of the Bible (commonly called the Pentateuch, or Book of Five Volumes) are supposed by most English readers of the Bible to have been written by Moses, except the last chapter of Deuteronomy, which records the death of Moses, and which (of course, it is generally allowed) must have been added by another hand (perhaps, that of Joshua)." With this statement, subject only to a presumption that a few notes were long subsequently incorporated with the original narrative (in order to clear up geographical and other matters, which had become somewhat obscure) by Ezra or some other of the inspired writers, the unlearned as well as men of learning are generally found to agree; but on the subject of what follows opinions are not so uniform. The bishop continues thus:—" It is believed, that Moses wrote under such special guidance and teaching of the Holy Spirit, that he was preserved from making any error in recording those matters which came within his own cognisance, and was instructed also in respect of events which took place before he was born—before, indeed, there was a human being on the earth to take note of what was passing: he was in this way, it is supposed, enabled to write a true account of the Creation. And, though the accounts of the Fall and of the Flood, as well as of later events which happened in the time of Abraham, Isaac, and Jacob, may have been handed down by tradition from one generation to another, and even some of them (perhaps) written down in words or represented in hieroglyphics, and Moses may (probably) have derived assistance from these sources also in the composition of his narrative, yet in all his statements, it is believed, he was under such constant control and superintendence of the Spirit of God, that he was kept from making any serious error and certainly from writing any thing altogether untrue." (Pp. 3 & 4.)

That this is a correct representation of the opinion of many men of learning whose views are entitled to our respectful attention is not to be denied: many deeply thinking Christians, however, do not yield it their unqualified assent. The writer of this remembers that, in his childhood, his parents, in answer to his inquiries as to how Moses knew about the Creation and the Flood and the other matters related in "Genesis" (all of which happened before Moses was born), told him that God gave him the information during the "forty days and forty nights" that he "was in the Mount," as recorded in Ex. xxiv. 18; and that Moses subsequently dictated it to Aaron and his sons and the seventy elders, to be written down by them. His parents (both of whom were persons of thought and of no little research) also informed him that, whenever any Jew had copied any portion of the Scriptures in the original Hebrew in which they were written, some angelic being had guided his pen to prevent his making a mistake even in the Copy; whence, there were no variations among the different copies of the Sacred Books. They, doubtless, supposed so at that time; but ere they died they knew otherwise. My investigations long since made me aware that the labors of Dr. Kennicott and others had fully proved that the various Hebrew copies of the books of the Old Testament had been subject to the same fate as has befallen all books that have been frequently copied—that one letter or word has been sometimes mistakenly written for another, that words and sentences have been omitted in some copies, and that words and even whole paragraphs have been inserted in others; yet these variations affect but a very small portion of the whole, and do not render doubtful any important statement. This, however, sufficiently disproves the fiction of no variations in the copies, and entirely overthrows the fable concerning angelical guidance of the writers' pens. In another direction, the writer's researches have led to his rejection of the opinion—that the information contained in "Genesis" was communicated to Moses in Mount Sinai, because he cannot find it so stated in the Sacred Record: nevertheless, he still believes the whole of "Genesis" to be an inspired composition. For, in the first place, Adam, Enoch, Noah, Abraham, Isaac, Jacob, and Joseph were all of them inspired persons, who received revelations from God; and there seems to be no reason for rejecting the opinion of the Jews, that these men recorded the events of their respective times: and, in the second place, if Moses made use of these records of the patriarchs, and moulded the whole into one composition (thus forming the first of his Five Volumes), the Book must still be held to be inspired, since the original writers and their copyist were alike under the divine influence. " For the prophecy came not in old time by the will of man, but holy men of God spake as they were moved by the Holy Ghost." (2 Pet. i. 21.)

The bishop next states (p. 5) that he " would most gladly have turned away from all such investigations as these" (*i.e.*, as to the truth of the narrative and the authorship of the books) ; adding " for myself I have become engaged in this inquiry from no wish or purpose of my own, but from the plain necessities of my position as a Missionary Bishop." It seems to me, that, before he first took upon himself the situation of a Minister of the Gospel, he ought to have satisfied himself of the truth upon these matters.

He thus states the conclusion he has arrived at, after he had made up his mind deliberately to undertake and had made the investigation :—" The result of my inquiry is this, that I have arrived at the conviction—as painful to myself at first as it may be to my reader, though painful now no longer under the clear shining of the Light of Truth—that the Pentateuch, as a whole, cannot possibly have been written by Moses, or by any one acquainted personally with the facts which it professes to describe ; and further that the so-called Mosaic narrative, by whomsoever written, and though imparting to us (as I fully believe it does) revelations of the Divine Will and Character, cannot be regarded as *historically true*." (P. 8.) How there can be *revelations of the Divine Will* imparted to us by a work, which, whilst itself pretending to be a faithful narrative of highly important events affecting by their results (if true) the whole human race, and claiming to be written under the guidance of the Holy Spirit, is thus deliberately declared to be *not historically true* (and must, as a consequence, be admitted to be a falsehood, as not being what it pretends to be) ?—is a question, the bishop's answer to which I leave to abler logicians than I am to prove: the logical method followed by myself would lead to a different conclusion.

The bishop hints that the difficulties, which have led to his conversion from a belief in the truth of the Mosaic narrative, are not those usual with infidels and sceptics; though he proceeds, with an evident zest for the subject, to enumerate the most prominent of the old standard objections (some of which, he tells us, " are of themselves very formidable "). He then proceeds (p. 9) to say—" They are not such, even, as are raised, when we regard the trivial nature of a vast number of conversations and commands ascribed directly to Jehovah, especially the multiplied ceremonial minutiæ laid down in the Levitical Law." If that Law be a revelation from Jehovah, and whether it be so or not is only to be decided by the settlement of the question as to the truthfulness of the accompanying historical narrative, there can be nothing *trivial* in it; and it appears to me, that, when the bishop made the assertion, he had not really considered the state of society in the East in ancient times: however, I am not called upon to prove or disprove anything here, as he admits that he is not going to depend on this. Next he says " They are not such, even, as must be started at once in most pious minds, when such words as these are read, professedly coming from the Holy and Blessed One, the Father and 'Faithful Creator' of all mankind,—' If the master [of a Hebrew servant] have given him a wife, and she have borne him sons or daughters, *the wife and her children shall be her master's*, and he shall go out free* by himself' (Ex. xxi. 4); the wife and children in such a case being placed under the protection of such other words as these,—' If a man smite his servant, or his maid, with a rod, and he die under his hand, he shall be surely punished: *notwithstanding*, if he continue a day or two, he shall not be punished; for *he is his money*' (Ex.

---

* The word "free" is not in our authorised version, but is implied from the context.

xxi. 20, 21). I shall never forget the revulsion of feeling, with which a very intelligent Christian native, with whose help I was translating these words into the Zulu tongue, first heard them as words said to be uttered by the same great and gracious Being, whom I was teaching him to trust in and adore. His whole soul revolted against the notion, that the Great and Blessed God, the Merciful Father of all Mankind, would speak of a servant or maid as mere 'money,' and allow a horrible crime to go unpunished, because the victim of the brutal usage had survived a few hours. My own heart and conscience at the time fully sympathized with his;* but I then clung to the notion, that the main substance of the narrative was historically true; and I relieved his difficulty and my own for the present, by telling him that I supposed that such words as these were written down by Moses, and believed by him to have been divinely given to him, because the thought of them arose in his heart (as he conceived) by the inspiration of God, and that hence to all such laws he prefixed the formula—'Jehovah said unto Moses,' without it being on that account necessary for us to suppose that they were actually spoken by the Almighty. This was, however, a very

---

* As Canon Stowell's remark, that the "bishop has been converted by a poor Zulu Kaffir," has been said to be an untruth; I would here observe that these words of the bishop prove its truth. What other meaning can be attached to the words, than that his mind was converted to the same opinion as that of the Zulu?

great strain upon the cord, which bound me to the ordinary belief in the historical veracity of the Pentateuch; and since then that cord has snapped in twain altogether." (Pp. 9 & 10.)

The reply to this passage of the bishop's will be necessarily somewhat lengthy. In the first place, the mode of government in the East, whether of the family and household or of the tribe or nation, has never been in accordance with our European notions. Trial by Jury, in our modern sense of the term, does not exist among them; but, the government being patriarchal and tribal, the head of a family is held to be responsible for every act of his wives and children and every individual member of his household, and the chief of a tribe is (in like manner) responsible to other tribes or to the general government for the acts of every individual under him. The power thus existing in the acknowledged head may be exercised by him even in questions of life or death, and there is no appeal from his decree; and, in many instances, there is no written law to guide them. This system has existed in the East from the earliest periods of which history furnishes us with any account. But, beside this, in ancient times we see several empires rear their lofty heads in the great cities, whose chieftains exercise despotic sway over their subjects, and are at continual war with their neighbours in order to extend their dominions and to satiate their lust of conquest. There is no check upon the ambition or the cruelty of the ruler; unless we regard as such the occasional assassination of the tyrant, either by some individual who may have had a private grievance to revenge, or by some commander in the tyrant's armies or some servant in his palace become ambitious to supplant him. The histories of Babylon and Assyria sufficiently prove this, and the subjects of the sculptures discovered in the present day among the ruins of Nineveh and elsewhere leave us no ground for doubting. Female chastity knew no protection, prostitution of the whole sex was a part of the state religion, and vices which one shudders to name were practised by the male portion of society without restraint. In Egypt, it is true, the priesthood interposed some little check on the despotic tendencies of the sovereign; but, even here, the sculptures and hieroglyphics still remaining on the walls of ruined palaces and temples and painted in the tombs, amid much that shows a more civilized state of domestic life, reveal to us (though slightly modified) the practice of the same cruelties and vice and debauchery as disgrace the early histories of Babylon and Nineveh. It will be seen, from what I have said, that recent discoveries only confirm the statements of Holy Writ. In the next place, we must bear in mind the whole tendency of the

Code of Judgements contained in the 21st, 22d, and 23d chapters of Exodus. This is the Theocratic Code, not "the Levitical Law," it must be remembered. If this be compared with the practices of all the nations by whom the Israelites were surrounded, its vast superiority over their laws (be they what they might) becomes apparent: neither Moses with all his learning, nor any human being in that day, unaided by the inspiration of God, could have risen to such a height above the common ideas prevalent in his time. Thirdly, the very part of the Code cited by the bishop is, let it be borne in mind, intended for the protection of the Hebrew (not the Israelitish) servant. That a state of bond-service has existed in the East from time immemorial is well known to the learned : the father of a family sold his children into a state of perpetual servitude, receiving money for them ; a man sold himself to a master to be maintained and protected by him, and the purchaser could (therefore) sell him to another master upon the like conditions ; a man found guilty of a crime could be sold into bondage ; and captives taken in war might be dealt with in the same manner. But the Theocratic Code (amongst other things) puts very great restraint upon these practices. The Hebrew servant could only sell himself for six years, in the first instance : in the seventh year he was to go out free for nothing. (Ex. xxi. 2.) If he had sold himself, being previously married, his wife was released at the same time as himself (*v.* 3). Next comes the condition, which has been the bishop's stumbling block; but the 5th and 6th verses inform us that the servant need not be separated from the wife whom his master had given him and the children she had borne him: he could bind himself in perpetuity to his master, but only by a public act of his own in the presence of the judges; and then his master had no power to separate the family: though, even in this case, the arrival of the year of jubilee set them all free, without any ransom-money being paid to the master. If this be compared with the further law on this subject contained in Deut. xv. 1—18,* we shall see that the Jewish Law on the subject of bondage was a law of mercy, to which no Christian nation has ever attained in its usages. It may be said, but why was not the master required, having given a wife to his servant, to set her free with him: the answer is—because he could not: he had already bound himself to the woman's father, when he bought his daughter, to become her protector (Ex. xxi. 7—11); and, con-

---

* Especially *v.* 13—15.—" And, when thou sendest him out free from thee, thou shalt not let him go away empty: thou shalt furnish him liberally out of thy flock, and out of thy floor, and out of thy wine-press: of that wherewith THE LORD thy God hath blessed thee thou shalt give unto him. And thou shalt remember that thou wast a bondman in the land of Egypt, and THE LORD thy God redeemed thee: therefore, I command thee this thing this day."

sequently, could not be released from that responsibility. If a man became a thief, and could not make restitution, he was liable to be sold as a slave (Ex. xxii. 3); but still this could only be for six years. " He that stealeth a man and selleth him, or if he be found in his hand—he shall surely be put to death." (Ex. xxi. 16.) Hear these things, ye nominal Christians of the so-called United States of America! and blush to think of your vile practices, and your pretended appeals to the Bible to support your hell-born system! As to the bishop's addition, when he talks of " mere money," it will be seen that the adjective is not warranted by the context: and the bishop's words about " horrible crime" and " brutal usage " are alike unwarranted ; for the master dared not inflict a greater punishment on his servant than the number of blows allowed to be inflicted on a criminal by the judges—" Forty stripes he may give him, and not exceed" (Deut. xxv. 3); and, if (in smiting his man-servant or his maid-servant) he struck the servant's eye and caused it to perish, or if he knocked out a tooth, the master was compelled to let the servant go free for the eye's or the tooth's sake (Ex. xxi. 26 & 27). And, in the last place, the bondman could be a witness as well as his master ; for the Jewish Law knew no distinction as to who might or who might not be a witness before the judges.

E

But the bishop's grand argument, which he has endeavoured to work out in his pages, is this—" The conviction of the unhistorical character of the so-called Mosaic narrative seems to be forced upon us, by the consideration of the many absolute *impossibilities* involved in it, when treated as relating simple matters of fact; and without taking account of any argument, which throws discredit on the story merely by reason of the miracles or supernatural appearances recorded in it, or particular laws, speeches, and actions ascribed in it to the Divine Being.. We need only consider well the statements made in the books themselves, by whomsoever written, about matters which they profess to narrate as facts of common history. * * * * * If we do this, we shall find them to contain a series of manifest contradictions and inconsistencies, which leave us, it would seem, no alternative but to conclude that main portions of the story of the Exodus, though based (probably) on some real historical foundation, yet are certainly not to be regarded as historically true." (P. 11.) Here, then, we have charges of "impossibilities" and "manifest contradictions and inconsistencies" hurled against the " main portions of the story," which, if they can be substantiated, will, I admit, leave me no alternative but to deny the truth of the Mosaic account, and (consequently) to destroy the basis of my belief in a revelation from God; for, if the statement be "not historically true," I cannot see of what value it can be to any one other than to deceive. As to the bishop's phrase "unhistorical," I cannot see how it can be logically applied to the Pentateuch. On the point of the bishop's conclusions I am at issue with him, because I deny his premises. What will be said, if I can shew (as I hope to do) that these *impossibilities* and *inconsistencies*, which he has been so industrious in collecting, are not chargeable upon the original writings of Moses; but are derived from the mistaken chronology attached to our English translation of the Scriptures, from (in a few instances) misapprehensions by the translators themselves of the meaning of the original, and (last, but not least) from the bungling expositions of commentators? If this can be shewn only in some of the more "prominent instances," surely the bishop ought to pause in his career, and undertake a reëxamination of his fancied points of difficulty with a reference to the Hebrew text alone.

The first point we have to consider, in an endeavour to do away with the charge of "absolute impossibilities" and "manifest contradictions and inconsistencies" in the Mosaic narrative, is derived from the account of "the Descent into Egypt," contained in the 46th chapter of Genesis; and this involves an examination of numerous circumstances connected with the previous life of the patriarch Jacob and the lives of his sons Judah and Joseph.

The bishop commences his attack (Chap. ii. § 19, p. 17) by a reference to Gen. xlvi. 12:—"And the sons of Judah—Er, and Onan, and Shelah, and Pharez and Zarah; but Er and Onan died in the land of Canaan: and the sons of Pharez were Hezron and Hamul." On this he remarks—"It appears to me to be certain, that the writer here means to say that Hezron and Hamul were *born in the land of Canaan,* and were among the 70 persons (including Jacob himself, and Joseph and his two sons), who *came into Egypt* with Jacob;" and with his conclusion I most cordially agree. And here it may not be out of place for me to remark, that "the Explanations of Expositors," which form the subject of the bishop's 3d Chapter (pp. 21—30), seem to me to be very weak attempts to explain away the obvious import of Moses's words; and to constitute an armoury for infidels, from which they may fill their quivers to be able to annoy believers: in consequence, his observations on the comments of Hävernick, Scott, Hengstenberg, Kurtz, and Pool appear to me to be fully warranted; and, if it be true (as it is stated by the bishop) that some of these are represented to be "the greatest modern champions of the ordinary view," I can only indorse his remark - that it is an "attempt to set aside the plain meaning of the Scripture." Undoubtedly, these expositors, having accepted the ordinary chronology, have then been unable to reconcile the words of the narrative of Judah's marriage and the circumstances of the births of his several chidren (Gen. xxxviii.) with the fact of the births of his two grandchildren before he went down into Egypt (Gen. xlvi. 12); and have, therefore, offered the ridiculous explanation—that these grandsons of Judah went down into Egypt in the loins of their father Pharez. I shall hereafter shew that the inability to reconcile the passages arises from a false system of chronology (supposed by its authors to be drawn out in accordance with Moses's statements) having been adopted in modern times; whilst, if Moses's own words be taken, the supposed impossibility completely disappears.

In the following Table I have exhibited the arrangement of the persons, constituting the Israelites (*i.e.*, Jacob and his children, grandchildren, and great-grandchildren), at the period of their assembling in Egypt immediately after the descent of Jacob (Gen. xlvi.) ; concerning which it is said—(*v*. 27) " All the souls of the house of Jacob" [" which came out of his loins"—*v*. 26], " which came into Egypt, were threescore and ten:"—

8 ver.	JACOB (*or* ISRAEL) ...	... ...	
Sons.	*Sons' Sons.*	*Sons' Grandsons.*	
9. REUBEN	Hanoch, Phallu, Hezron, Carmi	....	5
10. SIMEON	{ Jemuel, Jamin, Ohad, Jachin, Zohar, Shaul }	....	7
11. LEVI	Gershon, Kohath, Merari	....	4
12. JUDAH	Shelah, Pharez, Zarah	Hezron, Hamul (*Sons of Pharez*)	6
13. ISSACHAR	Tola, Phuvah, Job, Shimron	....	5
14. ZEBULUN	Sered, Elon, Jahleel	....	4
15. DINAH (*Daughter*)	....		1
,,	JACOB'S FAMILY BY LEAH		— 32
,,	Do., together with Jacob—33.		
16. GAD	{ Ziphion, Haggi, Shuni, Ezbon, Eri, Arodi, Areli }	....	8
17. ASHER	{ Jimnah, Ishuah, Isui, Beriah, Serah (*Asher's Daughter*) }	Heber, Malchiel (*Sons of Beriah*)	8
18.	JACOB'S FAMILY BY ZILPAH		— 16
20. JOSEPH	MANASSEH, EPHRAIM	....	
21. BENJAMIN	{ Belah, Becher, Ashbel, Gera, Naaman* Ehi, Rosh, Muppim, Huppim, Ard*.... }	......	11
22.	JACOB'S FAMILY BY RACHEL—14.		
23. DAN	Hushim	....	2
24. NAPHTALI	Jahzeel, Guni, Jezer, Shillem	....	5
25.	JACOB'S FAMILY BY BILHAH		— 7
26. " All the souls that came with Jacob into Egypt, which came out of his loins, besides Jacob's sons' wives—all the souls were threescore and six "			6
			7

---

* In Num. xxvi. 40, Ard and Naaman are said to be " the sons of Bela," which circumstance does not appear from the list of " the sons of Benjamin " in Genesis ; but the Hebrew word for " sons " includes all direct descendants.

That this was the exact number of the Israelites (*i.e.*, Jacob or Israel and his direct descendants), who came into Egypt (*i.e.*, were assembled together in Egypt at Jacob's descent), is confirmed by Ex. i. 5—" All the souls that came out of the loins of Jacob were 70 souls, for Joseph was in Egypt already;" and Deut. x. 22—" Thy fathers went down into Egypt with three score and ten persons." *Hebrew*—" In" (not " with") " 70 souls [נפש שבעים ב , *B' Sh b ó i m N p sh**] " descended thy fathers Metsreim†-wards." This was addressed to Israel alone: see *v.* 12 & 15.

The bishop remarks (p. 18)—" I assume, then, that it is absolutely undeniable—that the narrative of the Exodus distinctly involves the statement, that the 66 persons 'out of the loins of Jacob' mentioned in Gen. xlvi., *and no others,*

---

* For the benefit of those who are not acquainted with the Hebrew characters, I may state that the letters are read from right to left; but, in indicating the corresponding English letters, I have followed our usual practice and arranged them from left to right; and, as in some cases one Hebrew letter is represented by two English ones, I have left small spaces between the respective representative-sounds, and have indicated the commencement of each word by a Capital; also, wherever in the Hebrew two words are joined together, I have indicated the separation in the English letters by putting an apostrophe; and, in reading the English sounds, our vowel "*e*" must be supplied after every consonant except the final one in a word: thus—*B' Sh b ó i m* represents only 6 Hebrew characters, while the *B* is a separate word; the two words mean " in seventy," and may be read *Be Shebeho-im.*

† "Metsreim" is the Hebrew name of Egypt.

went down with him into Egypt." To the words, which I have marked in Italics, I demur; because I consider that the whole of his bond-servants (and they must have been numerous) went into Egypt with Jacob and his direct descendants; and this I believe to be implied by the words "and his household," when Moses tells us "Now these are the names of the children of Israel, who came into Egypt: every man and his household came with Jacob." (Ex. i. 1.) This I shall now proceed, at considerable length, to shew.

It will not be denied, I presume, that Jacob, although having no other landed possession in the country of Canaan than the field of Machpelah and the cave that was therein near Mamre (which his grandfather Abraham had purchased of Ephron the Hittite) and the parcel of a field near Shalem (which he himself bought of the children of Hamor), was, nevertheless, a man of no little importance in the land, having flocks and herds and much substance: now this implies, as a necessity, a large following of retainers or bond-servants. I have previously referred to the difference between the manners and customs, which have prevailed among the inhabitants of Eastern countries from the earliest historical times down to the present day, and the kind of civilization existing among the Western nations; and I have also pointed out that a state of bond-service has existed in the East from time immemorial. Next, we must bear in mind that Jacob was the heir or representative of the house of Abraham, and (therefore) was the possessor of the wealth of the tribe ; whilst Abraham himself was the head of the western Hebrews ; and, although commentators may have fallen into the mistake of supposing an Israelite and a Hebrew to be synonymous, yet they are by no means to be confounded. Every Israelite was a Hebrew; but every Hebrew was not an Israelite, though he might become one by adoption. I have previously hinted at this distinction, which is every where prevalent throughout the Pentateuch, but which strangely enough seems to have been entirely disregarded by expositors of the Scripture, whilst its non-recognition has entangled them in a net-work of difficulties and led them to weave a tissue of absurdities. Paul was " an Israelite of the tribe of Benjamin ;" but he also claims to go further back than Israel, for he was " of the seed of Abraham " (Rom. xi. 1) : he was not an Israelite by the adoption of his ancestor into the tribe of Benjamin, but he was such by birth, being a direct descendant of Abraham through the child of promise Isaac and his son Jacob. That Paul was able to trace his genealogy is clear ; for he says—" I might also have confidence in the flesh. If any other man thinketh that he hath whereof he might trust in the flesh, I more—circumcised the eighth day, of the stock of Israel, of the tribe of Benjamin, a Hebrew of the Hebrews." (Philip. iii. 4 & 5.) Some, probably, think this last expression of the apostle a mere figure of speech; but I do not believe that Paul was in the habit of using unnecessary expletives; he was too much in earnest in his Master's business to do that. We must here consider that the Hebrew language has no superlative form of a word, such as we have when we say "high, higher, highest;" and that their (the Hebrews') mode of expressing the idea was for "highest" to say "high of high-ones:" hence, the Scriptures abound in such phrases as "King of kings" (*i.e.*, the most exalted King), "Lord of lords" (*i.e.*, the highest Lord, one who is over all others), "the Holy of holies" (*i.e.*, the most holy place). With this consideration, we shall understand what St. Paul meant, when he called himself "a Hebrew of the Hebrews:" it was, that, amongst all of the Hebrew race, he was essentially a Hebrew—one, who could trace his descent directly from that branch of the race, which had been by God exalted to the heirship; not taken in by adoption. And this view is still further confirmed by the apostle's words, when he says—" For they are not all Israel, who are of Israel." (Rom. ix. 6.) Nevertheless, there were limitations to the Israelitish law of adoption, even among those of Hebrew race. Thus, the Ammonite or the

Moabite was excluded (although of Hebrew lineage) from the right of being adopted into the congregation of the Children of Israel (called " the Congregation of THE LORD ") unto the 10th generation (Deut. xxiii 3); the Edomite could be adopted into the congregation in the 3d generation, " for " (it is said) " he is thy brother ;" and the Egyptian was put upon the same footing, " because" (it is added) " thou wast a stranger in his land" (*v.* 7 & 8).

We now come to consider of whom the household of Abraham consisted, and how it was extended. " Abram," when he left the country of Haran with Lot, " took all their substance that they had gathered and the souls that they had gotten " (*i.e.*, the servants or followers whom they had purchased or had attached to themselves); " and into the land of Canaan they came." (Gen. xii. 5.) After residing in Canaan some time, he removed, in consequence of a famine, into Egypt ; and it is then said, that " he had sheep, and oxen, and he-asses, and men-servants, and maid-servants, and she - asses, and camels" (*v.* 16). When " Abram, and Lot with him," came back " out of Egypt into the south " of Canaan, taking with him " all that he had," we are told that he " was very rich in cattle, in silver, and in gold " (xiii. 1 & 2); " and Lot also," we are told, " had flocks, and herds, and tents" (*v.* 5). Next the Sacred Record informs us—" And the land was not able to bear them, that they might dwell together; for their substance was great, so that they could not dwell together: and there was a strife between the herdmen of Abram's cattle and the herdmen of Lot's cattle" (*v.* 6 & 7): this led to the friendly separation of Abram and his nephew. We have seen thus far that " Abram had gotten" (not " begotten ") " souls," that " he had " [was possessed of] " men-servants and maid-servants," and that there were " herdmen " in his service ; and, in addition to this he is described as being " very rich : " in fact, he, who had come " out of " his native " country," and had left his " kindred " and his " father's house," to come " unto a land, that (THE LORD had said) I will shew thee," was already become a great chief of his tribe: his name was known in Canaan and in Egypt, and he was already become great and was blessed ; whereby a portion of the first promise was fulfilled—" And I will make of thee a great nation. *and I will bless thee and make thy name great ;* and thou shalt be a blessing : and I will bless them that bless thee, and curse him that curseth thee : and in thee shall all families of the earth be blessed." (Gen. xii. 2 & 3.) But now a further promise was vouchsafed to him. Hitherto he has been the head of a wandering tribe : he is to become the possessor of a country, in which at present he owns not one foot of ground. He was in the south of Canaan, when THE LORD said unto him—" All the land which thou seest, to thee will I give it, and to thy seed for ever: and I will make thy seed as the dust of the earth; so that, if a man can number the dust of the earth, then shall thy seed also be numbered" (xiii. 15 & 16). Before he was to have a great name, and to become a blessing to others: now he is to have a country, which is to belong for ever to his own direct born (not adopted) heirs. He next enters into a league with the princes of the country; and soon afterwards we are introduced to an account of one of those raids of the tyrants of the East, to which I have previously alluded. (Gen. xiv.) When the four kings had overthrown the five at the battle in the Vale of Siddim, and carried off the prisoners (among whom was Lot, Abram's nephew); " there came one that had escaped, and told Abram the Hebrew; for he dwelt in the plain of Mamre the Amorite, brother of Eshcol and brother of Aner; and these were confederate with Abram: and, when Abram heard that his brother* was taken captive, he armed his trained servants, born in his own house, three hundred and eighteen; and pursued

---

* The Hebrew words rendered "brother" and "sister" mean any *male* or *female* *kinsman* or *kinswoman* respectively; and the word rendered "father" means also a *grandfather* or *great-grandfather*, or more remote *ancestor*.

them unto Dan: and he divided himself against them (he and his servants) by night, and smote them, and pursued them unto Hobah, which is on the left-hand of Damascus: and he brought back all the goods, and also brought again his brother Lot and his goods, and the women also and the people" (*v.* 13—16). Here Abram comes before us as the great captain of a conquering army and the prudent general: he is the head of a confederacy; but his own trained soldiers, of his own household and lineage, led forth by himself, amount to 318. Now this necessarily implies a far larger number of dependents, for none but men trained in the art of defence are included among the 318, and there are women and children besides: his own household, then, must have been to be counted by the thousand, and none of these were his own progeny. But, though Abram might well have claimed a reward from the natives of the country for the protection he had thus afforded them, he would receive no reward. "I have lifted up my hand unto THE LORD (the Most High God, the Possessor of Heaven and Earth), that I will not take from a thread even to a shoe-latchet; and that I will not take any thing that is thine; lest thou shouldst say 'I have made Abram rich'" (*v.* 22 & 23)—are the words of the generous chief to the king of Sodom, in whose behalf he had gained the victory and rescued his people from slavery. Abram had now become "a blessing."

Here, too, it should be remarked, that the epithet "the Hebrew" is applied to Abram (*v.* 13); which appears to have been the appellation of all the descendants of his ancestor Eber, mentioned in Gen. xi. 14—17, and x. 24 & 25. In the last passage, we are told that "unto Eber were born two sons; the name of one was Peleg (*i.e.*, division), for in his days was the earth divided; and his brother's name was Joktan." From Peleg Abram was descended; and from Joktan (called Kahtân by the Arabs) the southern Arabs of the elder branch claim to be descended. As the Arabs of the younger branch and the northern and eastern Arabs are descended from Ishmael or from Abraham's sons by Keturah, while the Bedâwî or Bedoweens probably include the remnants of the Edomites and Moabites and Ammonites (the former descended from Jacob's twin-brother Esau, and the two latter from Abram's nephew Lot); we see that the Arabs are Hebrews, though not Israelites. Before I quit this subject, there is one passage of Scripture more to be mentioned: it is "Unto Shem also, the father of all the Children of Eber, the brother of Japheth the elder—even to him were children born." (Gen. x. 21.) As the statements in this verse have been much controverted, and its obvious meaning has been attempted to be explained away, I shall supply a translation of the original, closely following the exact arrangement of the Hebrew:—

[*V'L'Sh m Yld Gm Hua Abi Kl Bni Aabr Ahhi Jpht H'Gdu l* ולשם ילד גם הוא אבי כל בני עבר אחי יפת הגדול]
"And to Shem *children** were-born: moreover, he [this] *is* ancestor *of* all *the* Children *of* Heber, brother *of* Japheth the ancient.†" Here, it is clear, a statement is made, which claims for Shem the distinction of being that one of the three Sons of Noah from whom the Hebrews [Benî Hêber] were descended; while we are also reminded that Japheth was the eldest brother of the three, the most honorable by rank and age. And yet, while pretending to acknowledge the Sacred Record, Baron Bunsen uses these expressions—" The historical meaning of Kham " [Ham] " is Egyptian. Khamitic is the first indistinct stage of Asiatic Semitism. This fact is symbolically represented by Kham, as Shem's elder brother, Japhet being the youngest of the three. Scripture calls Shem the elder brother of Japhet, but not of Kham." (" Outlines of the Philosophy of Universal History, applied to Language and Religion," vol. i., p. 190.) By what process of perverted ingenuity the Baron arrived at such a criticism of the words of Moses as is implied in the passage I have

---

* The words in Italics are implied, but not expressed, in the Hebrew; and the words "were-born" represent only one Hebrew word " *Y l d.*"

† *H'G d u l*, which I have rendered "the ancient," implies "the greater by age or birthright," as well as " the greater in rank or estimation," "the most dignified," "he who precedes all others." Well has he been called "Old Japheth."

here quoted I am uncertain; but I suspect that he has simply adopted the version of his countryman Von Bohlen, who has given the verse thus in his "Illustrations of Genesis"—"But sons were also born unto Shem, the elder brother of Japheth, who is the father of all the sons of Eber." Eng. ed., vol. ii., pp. 245-6. I can only characterize this as a vile mistranslation of the original. We have seen that the words "$A\,hh\,i\ J\,pht\ H'G\,d\,u\,l$" are the end of the sentence in the Hebrew; there being no article before $A\,hh\,i$ ('brother'), while the word $G\,d\,u\,l$ ('ancient' or 'elder') has the article H ('the') prefixed and is thus rendered emphatic, and immediately follows $J\,ph\,t$ ('Japheth'): hence, the adjective "elder" can only be referred to the name "Japheth," which closely precedes it. Had there been the article H ('the') also preceding $A\,hh\,i$ ('brother') [which is not the case], the translation of the passage might have been doubtful; but, as it is, the critic has no ground for doubting to whom the word "elder" should be referred.

We have seen that the name "Hebrew" was far older than the epithet "Israelite," and was far more comprehensive originally. We now return to the consideration of the household of Abram and God's covenants with him. Abram had been promised that he should have direct born heirs to inherit his property,

but this had not yet been fulfilled : he now addresses God thus—
"I go childless, and the steward of my house is this Eliezer of Damascus! Behold! to me Thou hast given no seed ; and, lo! one born in my house is mine heir!" (Gen. xv. 2 & 3.) To this it is replied—"This shall not be thine heir; but he, that shall come forth out of thine own bowels, shall be thine heir:" to which there is added—"Look now toward heaven, and tell the stars, if thou be able to number them : so shall thy seed be!" (*V*. 4 & 5.) He is afterwards foretold the history of his promised descendants for 400 years—that they should become strangers and servants in another country, where the inhabitants would afflict them ; but that, after residing there for four generations, they should come out thence "with great substance," and should return to inherit the land of the Amorites where Abram then dwelt. (*V*. 13—16.)

Still Abram has no child by his wife Sarai ; and he is 85 years old, and his wife about ten years younger : so, according to the custom of eastern countries, his wife gives him her bondwoman Hagar to be a second wife, and she bears Ishmael ; but this is not the child who is to inherit the land and his father's wealth, and to be the head of all the Hebrew peoples. After thirteen years a further promise is made to Abram : God makes a covenant with him, changes his name to Abraham and his wife's name to Sarah, and appoints the rite of circumcision. (Gen. xvii.) Among the promises now made we find—" I will make thee exceeding fruitful; and I will make nations of thee, and kings shall come out of thee: and I will establish My covenant between Me and thee and thy seed after thee in their generations for an everlasting covenant, to be a God unto thee and to thy seed after thee: and I will give unto thee and to thy seed after thee the land wherein thou art a stranger, all the land of Canaan, for an everlasting possession; and I will be their God" (v. 6—8). The rite of circumcision is appointed to be "a token of the Covenant" between God and Abraham; and God ordains "He that is eight days old shall be circumcised among you, every man-child in your generations; he that is born in the house, or bought with money of any stranger, who is not of thy seed: he that is born in thy house, and he that is bought with thy money, must needs be circumcised; and My covenant shall be in your flesh for an everlasting covenant: and the uncircumcised man-child, whose flesh is not circumcised, that soul shall be cut off from his people; he hath broken my covenant" (v. 12—14). Abraham is then told that Ishmael is not the promised seed; but that Sarah shall have a son, who is to be called Isaac; and God adds "My covenant will I establish with Isaac" (v. 21): this is the promised seed. Abraham does not wait till the promised child is born, but proceeds at once to obey the directions: Abraham himself (at the age of 99), Ishmael his son (now 13 years old), and " every male among the men of Abraham's house "—all are " circumcised in the self-same day " (*v.* 23—27). Here we find that all of Abraham's household—every male among his numerous retainers, whether born of his lineage or purchased from foreigners, is introduced into the Covenant, nine months before the birth of him who is to become the head of the house and the inheritor of all the property.

We do not require to trace the further progress of the household of Abraham; having already fully established its great extent, with the including of the whole under the Covenant, to be subject to the heir appointed. In due time, Isaac was born; and, when 40 years old, was married to Rebekah, who was an eastern Hebrew and the grand-daughter of his father's brother: she, 20 years after their marriage, bore him twins — Esau and Jacob. Three years before Isaac was married, his mother Sarah died at the age of 127; but Abraham survived her 40 years, and lived to see Isaac's sons nearly attained to manhood. Moreover, Abraham had had six sons by another wife Keturah; and, " while yet he lived," he " gave gifts " to these, " and sent them away from

Isaac his son eastward unto the East country:" he then "gave all that he had unto Isaac:" at length, having attained the age of 175 years, he died; "and his sons Isaac and Ishmael buried him in the cave of Machpelah," which he had purchased to bury Sarah his wife in. (Gen. xxv. 1—10.) Ishmael survived his father 48 years, and died at the age of 137; having had twelve sons, who became the princes of as many tribes of Arabs: these are the Ishmaelites, from whom the Arabs of the present day deem it an honor to be able to trace descent. Isaac survived Abraham 105 years, and died at Mamre or Hebron (the place of his birth) at the age of 180; and there "his sons Esau and Jacob buried him." Esau is the ancestor of the Edomites, and Jacob of the Israelites; and these [the last mentioned] became the principal of all the Hebrew peoples. "Esau dwelt in Mount Seir" (Gen. xxxvi. 8), which stretched from the N.E. of the Peninsula of Sinai as far as the southern part of the Dead Sea; while the sons of Ishmael "dwelt from Havilah unto Shur, that is before Egypt as thou goest toward Assyria" (Gen. xxv. 18), thus occupying the northern parts of the country of Arabia from the Isthmus of Suez to the mouth of the Euphrates and head of the Persian Gulf. It will be well hereafter to bear in mind the fact, that all of these were Hebrews, and as such could be readily incorporated among the followers of the Children of Israel.

A few circumstances of the life of Isaac require to be briefly referred to. Though Abraham, in sending away to the eastward his children by Keturah, very probably gave a portion of his followers to them; and it would also seem very likely, that others would be attached to the leadership of Ishmael; yet the headship of the western Hebrews remained with Isaac. One of those famines, which appear to have been not very unfrequent in the south of the Holy Land, having occurred; Isaac is warned by God not to go down into Egypt, nor to quit the country; and God's promise to Abraham is renewed to Isaac. (Gen. xxvi. 1—5.) He removes his tent, however, from Lahai-roi near Hebron, in the land of the Amorites; and pitches it in Gerar, in the land of the Philistines. Having thus removed the head-quarters of his tribe, he, with the consent of the king of that part of the country, sowed the ground, and reaped a plentiful harvest: and it is said, that "he became very great; for he had possession of flocks, and possession of herds, and great store of servants" (*v.* 13 & 14): and, in consequence, the Philistines both envied and feared him; and their king "Abimelech said unto Isaac, 'Go from us, for thou art much mightier than we'" (*v.* 16). Isaac removed southerly, and dug and opened wells in the desert; and, for the possession of some of these, the Philistine herdmen strove with Isaac's herdmen; but Isaac was not a man of warlike habits, and he relinquished the wells he had opened, and removed still further south into the desert, where his servants digged another well. (*V.* 17—25.) King Abimelech becomes afraid for the consequences of the acts of his subjects; and proceeds to Isaac's head-quarters, accompanied by a friend and the chief captain of his army: there peace is established, a covenant is entered into, a feast is made, and an oath is taken—all vividly reminding us of the exact resemblance with the practices of the pastoral tribes of Syria and Arabia in the present day. Isaac's head-quarters thus became the original of the city of Beer-sheba [*i.e.*, the Well of the Oath]. (*V.* 26—33.) Isaac was more inclined to meditation than to the undertaking of any stirring actions : hence, his leadership of the tribe was not likely to attract followers, but rather to diminish them.

The circumstances recorded in the 27th chapter of Genesis, concerning the manner in which Jacob supplanted his twin-brother Esau in the birth-right, and secured his father Isaac's blessing, are well known. In that blessing Isaac used these words—" Let people serve thee, and nations bow down to thee ! be lord over thy brethren, and let thy mother's sons bow down to thee ! cursed be every one that curseth thee, and blessed be he that blesseth thee!" (*V.* 29.) Here we have the headship of the tribe given to

Jacob: " thy brethren " could not mean Esau alone, but must be used in the extended sense of the word for all those of the Hebrew race who followed Jacob's father, and in the term "thy mother's sons" all of his brother's future descendants would be included; and this is subsequently confirmed by Isaac's words to Esau — "Behold! I have made him thy Lord, and all his brethren have I given to him for servants." (*V.* 37.) This led to enmity between the two brothers, and Esau threatened Jacob's life. Esau having married two Canaanitesses; Rebekah dreaded lest her beloved son Jacob should do the like, and induced Isaac to send him away to Haran in Padan-Aram (the country of the eastern Hebrews), there to seek a wife of the house of Jacob's uncle Laban, the brother of Rebekah. The period of Jacob's residence in Padan-Aram has been commonly supposed to have been twenty years, and so bishop Colenso seems to have taken it; but I shall hereafter shew that its duration was full 40 (not 20) years: at present I am tracing the "household."

While Jacob dwelt among the tribe of the eastern Hebrews, called by the Sacred writer בני קדם [*B n i Q d m*], "the Children of the East" or "the Eastern People" (Gen. xxix. 1), he married two sisters (his cousins) and their two bond-women, by whom he had a family of eleven sons and a daughter in Padan-Aram, and a twelfth son was born after his return to Canaan. He, who had passed over the Jordan a leafless branch of his father's house, with his staff in his hand, had "become two bands," when he returned to his native country. (Gen. xxxii. 10.) We are told, even while he was in Padan-Aram, that "the man increased exceedingly; and had much cattle, and maid-servants, and men-servants, and camels, and asses." (Gen. xxx. 43.) Here we see Jacob with great wealth and a large following, not derived even from any property given him by his father, but entirely acquired by himself (under the Divine blessing) during his absence from home: he had as yet inherited nothing of the property of his own tribe, for his father Isaac was still alive. His household was very numerous, in addition to his four wives and their children; and they [the followers] were of the eastern Hebrews, many (at least) of whom were semi-idolaters. Laban, we know, was such; and, when Jacob was living at Beth-El, after his return to Canaan, he "said unto his household and to all that were with him, 'Put away the strange gods that are among you!' and they gave unto Jacob all the strange gods which were in their hand, and all their ear-rings which were in their ears; and Jacob hid them under the oak which was by Shechem." (Gen. xxxv. 1—4.) Thus was the worship of idols extinguished by him among the Hebrews whom he had brought with him from Padan-Aram; and these were subsequently incorporated with the western branch of the race, when Jacob succeeded to the government of the tribe, on the death of his father Isaac, at which time Jacob was 120 years old. Jacob had only possessed the headship 10 years, when the Descent into Egypt took place; and the circumstances which I have previously detailed being well considered, little doubt can remain that the tribe was then to be numbered by thousands; and these constituted the household of Jacob and the households of his sons, when they had the land of Goshen assigned to them as a residence, by the king of Egypt, after their descent.

It may be objected, however, that the tribe had been greatly diminished during Jacob's absence from Canaan and before he took the headship; and that Esau, having remained at home, and knowing that he was not to inherit, would have sought to attract the bulk of the tribe to his leadership. But this was not so. Esau in his younger days delighted in hunting, a pursuit not likely to attract a numerous train, as the followers would gain little thereby. As he grew older, however, Esau, perceiving that his marriage with two Hittite wives was displeasing to his parents, married Bashemath, his uncle Ishmael's daughter; and was likely thereby to have attracted some of the Ishmaelites to his following, they being of a more wandering and warlike disposition than the tribe who belonged to his father Isaac. When Jacob returned from Padan-Aram, he sent his messengers to his brother Esau (who already at that time had gone away from his father, and was dwelling in the land of Seir), with a present of " 200 she-goats and 20 he-goats, 200 ewes and 20 rams, 30 milch-camels with their colts, 40 kine and 10 bulls, 20 she-asses and 10 foals," to propitiate his brother; and it was, whilst awaiting the result of the present he had sent forward, that Jacob had the remarkable wrestling, which resulted in the change of his name to "Isra-el" (*i.e.*, a Prince of God). (Gen. xxxii.) Esau came forth, accompanied by 400 men, to meet his brother Jacob: at first, he refused to accept the present, because (he said) " I have enough, my brother!" but, being still urged, he took it. (Gen. xxxiii.) A most ample reconciliation took place, and all enmity between the brothers was for ever extinguished. When Isaac "died and was gathered unto his people," his two sons buried him. Esau, at once, acknowledged his brother's right to the headship of the tribe: " And Esau took his wives and his sons and his daughters, *and all the persons of his house*, and his cattle, and all his beasts, and all his substance, which he had got in the land of Canaan; and went into the country from the face of his brother Jacob ; for their riches were more than that they might dwell together ; and the land wherein they were strangers could not bear them, because of their cattle." (Gen. xxxvi. 6 & 7.) Here we have sufficient proof that a man's "house" consisted of other persons beside himself and his wives and children.

The western Hebrews now consisted of three tribes—Ishmaelites, Edomites, and Israelites ; but the last named was acknowledged to be the head or the royal tribe, and these must have followed Jacob and his sons into Egypt. It were folly to suppose, that the ruling house would or could desert their followers, when they shifted their head-quarters from the land of Canaan to the land of Goshen in consequence of the Famine : but the Sacred Record removes all ground for doubting, for it tells us—" Then Joseph came and told Pharaoh, and said ' My father and my brethren, and their flocks and their herds, *and all that they have*, are come out of the land of Canaan ; and, behold ! they are in the land of Goshen ' " (Gen. xlvii. 1): and afterwards we are told—" And Joseph placed his father and his brethren, and gave them a possession in the land of Egypt, in the best of the land, in the land of Rameses, as Pharaoh had commanded : and Joseph nourished his father and his brethren, *and all his father's household*, with bread, according to their families " (*v.* 11 & 12). I have, I think, now sufficiently established it as a fact—that Moses's words imply that a very large number of persons went down into Egypt, beside the 70 individuals named in the 46th chapter of Genesis. The ruling family ("the promised seed," be it remembered) had not yet, however, attained to be numbered "as the stars of heaven," nor were their followers of their own lineage at present become innumerable "as the dust of the earth." Four generations of men had yet to pass, 215 years were to roll over their heads, during which the rulers and their followers were to become bond-men and bond-women, and to endure hard bondage, ere they were to be redeemed from their servitude by THE LORD their God, and led forth out of Egypt to return and possess the Promised Land; when the 70 were to have increased to 3,550 men of "twenty years old and upward," and their followers of the same race with themselves were to be estimated at 600,000 men capable of bearing arms.

Having disposed of one of the bishop's objections, I proceed to another. It is contained in Chap. ii. § 20, pp. 18 & 19; and is as follows:—

"Now Judah was *forty-two* years old, according to the story, when he went down with Jacob into Egypt. But, if we turn to Gen. xxxviii., we shall find that, in the course of these 42 years of Judah's life, the following events are recorded to have happened:—(1) Judah grows up, marries a wife 'at that time' (*v.* 1), that is, after Joseph's being sold into Egypt, when he was '17 years old' (Gen. xxxvii. 2), and when Judah, consequently, was (at least) *twenty* years old; and has, separately, three sons by her. (2) The eldest of these three sons grows up, is married, and dies: the second grows to maturity (suppose in another year), marries his brother's widow, and dies: the third grows to maturity (suppose in another year still), but declines to take his brother's widow to wife: she then deceives Judah himself, conceives by him, and in due time bears him twins, Pharez and Zarah. (3) One of these twins also grows to maturity, and has two sons (Hezron and Hamul) born to him, before Jacob goes down into Egypt.

"The above being certainly incredible, we are obliged to conclude that one of the two accounts must be untrue. Yet the statement, that Hezron and Hamul were born in the land of

Canaan, is vouched so positively by the many passages above quoted, which sum up the '70 souls,' that to give up this point is to give up an essential part of the whole story. But, then, this point cannot be maintained, however essential to the narrative, without supposing that the other series of events had taken place before hand, which we have seen to be incredible."

Had Moses stated what Bishop Colenso says is stated in the Sacred Narrative, it would " certainly " be " incredible " ; and the Book, in which such things were told, could not be accepted as a Revelation from God ; but Moses has not made such statements, even though Kurtz and Hengstenberg and numerous German and other critics think it to be so. The bishop's two first assumptions are untrue : Judah was more than 42 years old, at the time of the Going-down into Egypt ; and the phrase " at that time," quoted by the bishop, has no reference to the circumstance in the life of Joseph mentioned in the previous (37th) chapter : hence, the impossibility does not exist in the Sacred Record. This I now proceed to shew.

The bishop, in order to support his assertion as to Judah's age, inserts this note (p. 18)—" Joseph was 30 years old, when he ' stood before Pharaoh ' as governor of the land of Egypt,

Gen. xli. 46; and from that time 9 years elapsed (7 of plenty and 2 of famine), before Jacob came down to Egypt. At that time, therefore, Joseph was 39 years old. But Judah was about three years older than Joseph; for Judah was born in the *fourth* year of Jacob's double marriage, Gen. xxix. 35, and Joseph in the *seventh*, Gen. xxx. 24—26, xxxi. 41. Hence, Judah was forty-two years old, when Jacob went down to Egypt." In quoting the bishop's words, I have put in figures all his numbers of which I approve; but to those in words I cannot agree, because they are not found in the Bible, though the bishop asserts that they are. Here we are at issue on a plain matter of fact. Let the reader, then, refer to a copy of our English version which is not accompanied by any marginal notes. The quotations from the 29th and 30th chapters positively contain no numerical statements whatever, and the quotation from the 31st chapter contains no reference to the births of any of his children: the last quotation, however, does contain a numerical statement; and the meaning of this the bishop has mistaken, misled himself by the Chronology of Archbishop Usher, which has been attached (without sufficient authority for its support) to those copies of our authorised version that are supplied with marginal readings. The dates being in years B.C. (*i.e.*, before Christ), it is at once evident, cannot have been Moses's. If, now, we refer to one of the last mentioned copies, we shall find in the margin the following dates set against the births of Leah's first four sons, mentioned in Gen. xxix. 32, 33, 34, & 35 respectively:—Reuben, *circiter* 1752 B.C.; Simeon, *cir.* 1751; Levi, *cir.* 1750; and Judah, *cir.* 1749. Since the marriage of Jacob with Leah is, by the same authority (*i.e.*, the marginal chronology), set down as having occurred in 1753 B.C.; we perceive how the bishop arrived at his conclusion, that " Judah was born in the *fourth* year of Jacob's double marriage ;" he having also assumed that Jacob was married to Rachel almost immediately after his marriage to Leah, which has been supposed to be the case (although Moses's words shew 7 years to have intervened) in order to bolster up the requirements of the absurd chronology that has been adopted. Here we have proof of the bishop's first mistake, which he has sought to father upon Moses, with what support the reader can now judge.

Again, if we refer to the same authority (*i.e.*, the version with marginal readings), we shall find against Gen. xxx. 22—24, *cir.* 1745 B.C. set as the date of Joseph's birth, being (according to this chronology) the 8th year or 7 years complete from the assumed date of the marriage. This is the second error, which the bishop has fallen into and then fathered upon Moses. Next, as Joseph was, at least, $(30 + 7 + 2 =)$ 39 complete years old at the time of his father's coming into Egypt, while the bishop reckons, as above, $(7 — 4 =)$ 3 years for the excess of the age of Judah above that of Joseph ; he has fixed the age of Judah, when he accompanied his father into Egypt, at $(39 + 3 =)$ 42 years; and, then, asserted that Moses has said so.

I shall now proceed to tabulate the marginal chronology; and shew its thorough unlikelihood, from its non-agreement with our every-day experience concerning the usual intervals between the successive births of children from the same mother ; and the outrageous construction thereby put upon Moses's words in Gen. xxix.—xxxi.

                                                                                        Chap.   Ver.

Circiter 1760 B.C. Jacob (at the age of 77 *) goes to Haran, resides with his uncle Laban, and agrees to live in his house as a servant for 7 years, at the end of which time his cousin Rachel is to be given to him as a wife as "wages".. .. .. 29.   1—2

      * The age of Jacob at the time of his going to Haran is not stated by Moses : it is a mere inference from imperfect data.

1753.   Laban deceives Jacob ; and gives him his eldest daughter Leah as a wife, instead of Rachel .. ..   21—2

,,   Laban then gives Rachel to Jacob as a 2d wife, upon condition that he shall serve him a second period of 7 years .. ..   27—3

      This is irreconcileable with Moses's words ; for his statement is---that, in reply to Jacob's remonstrance (v. 25), " ' What is this

Ch. V.

thou hast done unto me? did not I serve with thee for Rachel? wherefore, then, hast thou beguiled me?' Laban said 'It must not be so done in our country, to give the younger before the first-born: fulfil her" [Rachel's] "week! * and we *will give thee this also,* for the service which thou shalt serve with me yet seven other years'" (v. 26 & 27): and then it is added, that "Jacob did so, and *fulfilled her week;* and he" [Laban] "gave him" [Jacob] "Rachel his daughter to wife also" (v. 28). Moses here clearly states that seven years elapsed after the first marriage before the second marriage took place.

* מלא שבע זאת [*M la Shbó Zat*] is literally "Fulfil seven *for* this-woman!" The word rendered "week" in our version is the Hebrew numeral "seven."

1752 B.C.	Leah bears Reuben		29.	32.
1751.	,, ,, Simeon			33.
1750.	,, ,, Levi			34.
1749.	,, ,, Judah, and leaves bearing			35.

According to this chronology, then, we have a woman bearing 4 children in 4 successive years—a not impossible circumstance, but a very unusual one; and a statement not to be fathered upon the Sacred Writer, unless his words be very clear to that effect, which certainly cannot be shewn.

,,	Rachel finding herself barren, at the end of 4 years from the double marriage, upbraids her husband, and then gives him her hand-maid Bilhah as a 3d wife	30.	1—4.
1748.	Bilhah bears Dan		5 & 6.
1747.	,, ,, Naphtali		7 & 8.

Here, again, we have the unusual circumstance of a second woman bearing 2 children in 2 successive years after her marriage, fathered upon Moses's words without any such statement being made by him

1749.	Leah finding that she has left bearing, in the same year in which she has given birth to Judah, gives her husband her hand-maid Zilpah as a 4th wife		9.

88

		Ch.
Circiter 1748 B.C.	Zilpah bears Gad	30.
1747.	,, ,, Asher	

Here, again, we have the unusual circumstance of a third woman bearing 2 children in 2 successive years after her marriage, fathered upon Moses's words without any such statement being made by him: and this, too, in the very same years that another woman has been the subject of the like unlikelihood.

1748. Leah having ceased to bear children for a whole year after the birth of Judah, in consequence of her husband keeping himself wholly to her sister (his 2d wife)'s tent, although the 4th wife has become the mother of a son to her husband in her (Leah's) tent in the mean time, bargains with her sister Rachel, by means of the mandrakes which her (Leah's) son Reuben (now aged 4 years) has found and brought to his mother, that her husband shall return to her (Leah's) tent for one night .. ..

In consequence of which,

1747.	Leah bears Issachar .. ..
1746.	,, ,, Zebulun .. ..
1745.	,, ,, Dinah (Daughter) .. ..

Here, again, we have Leah, after leaving bearing for one year, becoming the mother of 3 children in 3 successive years; having, according to the marginal chronology (which is certainly not the work of Moses), had 7 children at as many different births within 8 years from her marriage.

,,	Rachel bears Joseph (after 7 years of barrenness) ..	
1729.	,, ,, Benjamin* (having ceased bearing for 16 years), and dies in child-birth near Ephrath or Beth-lehem	35.

* The birth of Benjamin is placed (by this stupid chronology) 10 years after the return from Padan-Aram, and in the same year that Joseph was sold by his brethren to the Midianites and taken to Egypt; yet Moses represents Joseph as calling upon his brother Benjamin to recognise him at their (according to this chronology) first time of meeting after the year of Benjamin's birth (Gen. xlv. 12); and (by the same chronology) Benjamin is represented as being the father of 10 sons and grandsons when he was but 22 years of age.

Still further to shew the absurdity of the usually received chronology, I shall exhibit it in another form :—

```
1753 B.C.  Jacob (aged 84) marries 2 wives—Leah and Rachel.
1752.               Reuben born.
1751.               Simeon  do.
1750.               Levi    do.
1749.               Judah   do.
  ,,       Jacob (aged 88) marries Bilhah and Zilpah.
1748.                               Dan born.     Gad born.
1747.               Issachar born.  Naphtali do.  Asher do.
1746.               Zebulun do.
1745.               Dinah   do.    .. .. .. .. ..   Joseph born.
```

All of this is represented as having occurred within 8 years; and this absurdity is maintained by expositors of the Scripture, with manifest violence to the plain meaning of Moses's own words; because they have fallen into the mistake of supposing that Moses wrote annals (*i.e.*, that every event mentioned by him is recorded exactly in the same order as the sequence of the occurrence of the events), instead of his having written a history, in which each episode of the narrative is made complete by itself before proceeding to another narration, some portions of the events of which may have occurred before the termination of the preceding account. In consequence, it has been assumed that the events mentioned in Gen. xxx. 25—43, all occurred after the births of the 11 sons and a daughter, within the six years referred to in Gen. xxxi. 41; and further that the 20 years spoken of by Jacob, Gen. xxxi. 38, are the same as the 20 years spoken of in v. 41; the only statement to countenance this tissue of absurdities and violence to all the rest of Moses's account being the words in our authorised version—" And it came to pass, when Rachel had born Joseph, that Jacob said unto Laban 'Send me away, that I may go unto mine own place and to my country! Give me my wives and my children, for whom I have served thee ; and let me go! for thou knowest my service, which I have done thee.'" (Gen. xxx. 25 & 26.) As Bishop Colenso seems to be still fond of his mathematical studies, he might exercise himself with the calculation of the degree of probability there can be, that Moses (or whoever else it might be that compiled the Pentateuch) could be such an arrant fool as to attach such a string of very unlikely circumstances, combined with several natural impossibilities, to a tale, which (whether it be true or false) the writer has represented as a true narrative of matters of fact; or whether it is not the more probable circumstance, that the expositors and chronologers have made the statements of Moses appear ridiculous, by their *darkening counsel by words without knowledge.*

Before I proceed to analyze the words of Moses, it will be necessary to offer a few remarks on the manner in which Hebrew M.SS. were formerly written, and to give some explanations as to the usage of particular words in the ancient language, in order that such of my readers as are not familiar with the subject may be prepared to follow my argument. Hebrew M.SS. were anciently written (and all Synagogue Rolls of the Scriptures are still so written) without any distinction of words or sentences; the number of letters in a line being made the same throughout one M.S., and there being no punctuation or marks to indicate pauses in reading. It may be supposed, that, in consequence of such a system of writing, the meaning of large portions of books so written would be unintelligible, or (at least) very liable to be misunderstood; but it is not so. A large proportion of the vowel-sounds of the Hebrew is considered to be inherent in the consonants, and three letters generally constitute a word, while 5 letters (k, m, n, p, and ts) are made of a very different form when they end a word from what is used when they occur at the beginning or in the middle of a word. In addition to this, the letter ו [u or v], constituting a word of itself, but always joined to the beginning of the next word, very frequently marks the beginning of a phrase or a sentence; and thus affords a sure indication to assist in arranging the letters into words in reading. The same letter at the end of a word generally constitutes the personal pronoun "him" as an objective, or the adjective pronoun "his" as a possessive. For example, in the first 9 verses of the 28th chapter of Genesis, the letter ו [*u* or *v*] occurs 51 times in the Hebrew—22 times at the beginning of a word, 18 at the end of a word, and 11 in the middle of a word. In 20, of the 22 instances in which it occurs at the beginning of a word, our translators have rendered it by "and:" in the two remaining cases, they have rendered it "when" (*v.* 6) and "then." (*v.* 9). In 14 cases, of the 18 where it occurs at the end of a word, it means "him" or "his"; and, in the 4 other instances, it is the last letter of the proper name "Esau." Hence, despite of the absence of any divisions of the letters in the M.SS. into words and sentences, there is not so much difficulty for an educated person to understand Hebrew as there would at first seem to be; and the number of cases, where a false division of the letters into words and sentences is liable to happen, is comparatively few: nevertheless, there are some; and the passage in Gen. xxx. 22—26, to which I have before referred, is one of those where very different meanings will attach to the words, according to the division we adopt. When, soon after the invention of printing, the Jews began to print their Scriptures, they introduced a mode of division (of course, traditional with them) into their printed copies, which did not exist in their M.SS. ; and marked the endings of their verses by a point similar to our colon [:] : but these divisions are sometimes made without attending to the sense, and frequently seem to have been regulated by the mode of intonation in their public reading of the Scriptures, or by the number of words that a man could read aloud till he required to pause to draw breath. For instance, Gen. x. 15—18 is thus pointed in Hebrew Bibles :—" And Canaan begat Sidon his first-born and Heth : And the Jebusite and the Amorite and the Girgasite : And the Hivite and the Arkite and the Sinite : And the Arvadite and the Zemarite and the Hamathite and afterward were the families of the Canaanites spread abroad : "

The Hebrew language has only two tenses, or variations to express the time of an action or occurrence : hence the niceties known in our language to discriminate the exact relation of past events (such as " he was going, he went, he has gone, he had gone ") are not found in the Hebrew ; but must be inferred by comparing the different portions of the sentence or narration together. In giving a version of Hebrew in any other language, this is a matter of no small importance : it is, therefore, the duty of a translator carefully to attend to the context as well as to the phrase or sentence he is immediately translating, and to see that he construes the whole of a narration consistently, so as not to make his author appear to have written nonsense. By the matter and manner of Bishop Colenso's criticisms, it is evident that he has not attended to this rule ; but has sought whether he cannot strain the author's words, so as to make him appear ridiculous. Again, the Hebrew particle ו [*u* or *v*], to which I have previously referred, has the general meaning of adding something to what precedes: it is, accordingly, most frequently represented in English by " and ; " but sometimes it implies an addition by way of contrast, and must then be represented by " or " or " but : " when it commences a new episode in a narration, in addition to a preceding tale, it should be rendered " now ; " and the subordinate added parts of such a narration require it to be translated (as we have already seen) by " then " and " when," or (even in some cases) by the conjunction " that." I shall now analyze some of the statements of the Sacred Text.

In Gen. xxx. 22—24, we have this statement—" And God remembered Rachel ; and God hearkened to her, and opened her womb: and she conceived, and bare a son; and said 'God hath taken away my reproach:' and she called his name Joseph,* and said 'THE LORD shall add* to me another son.'" The two following verses contain this account—"And it came to pass, when Rachel had born Joseph, that Jacob said unto Laban 'Send me away, that I may go unto mine own place and to my country! Give me my wives and my children, for whom I have served thee; and let me go! for thou knowest my service, which I have done thee.'" (*V.* 25 & 26.) This translation is undoubtedly made, not only in accordance with the modern Hebrew punctuation, but also with an ancient traditional mode of dividing the sentences (for it seems to have been followed by the LXXII. in their Greek translation, though this is not absolutely certain). I shall now give the 24th & 25th verses as they appear in Hebrew M.SS., except that I shall separate the letters into words; for as to the words themselves there is no dispute; the difference being in the punctuation, which is certainly not due to Moses.

ותקרא את שמו יוסף לאמר יסף יהוה לי בן אחר
rhha nb il hvhJ phssj rmal phssuJ umsh ta arqtV

ויהי כאשר ילדה רחל את יוסף ויאמר יעקב אל
la bqaaJ rmayV phssuJ ta lhhR hdly rshak yhyv

* See Note on next page.

ולארצי   אל מקומי   ואלכה   שלחני   לבן
i tsralv   i muqm   la   hklav   in hhlsh   nbL

And she-called to name his Joseph, for to-say 'Will-add
V'   tqra   at shm 'u   Jussph l'   amr   jssph *

Jehovah to me son another:' and it-was as-to what-time
Jhvh   l' i bn   ahhr   v'   yhy   k'   ashr

gave-birth Rachel to Joseph. Now had-said Jacob to Laban
yldh   Rhhl at Jussph   V'   yamr   Jaaqb al Lbn

'Dismiss me, and I-will-go to dwelling my and to land my.'
shlhh 'ni   v'   alkh   al   mqum 'i   v' l' arts 'i

In the above translation, I have followed the exact arrangement of the words in the Hebrew; and I now give the translation in the usual sequence of English words:—

And she called his name Joseph, for she said " Jehovah will add to me another son ; " and this was when Rachel bare Joseph. Now Jacob had said to Laban " Send me away, and I will return to mine own home and to mine own country ! "

The meaning of this arrangement of the words is—that Rachel, in giving her son a name, considered that she was now

---

* יסף [*J ss ph*] is both "hath added" and "will add." יוסף [*Ju ss ph*] is the participle "adding" and the substantive "addition," from the same verb.

truly become a mother : before she had brought up her husband's children by her own bond-woman, born in her own tent, as her children : now she says "Jehovah *has added* to those, whom I have previously counted as mine, one who is truly mine own ; and I accept this as an omen from God, that I *shall* yet *add* to the number : " and this prophecy was uttered by her, at the time that she gave birth to Joseph. What follows is the commencement of a new episode in the life of Jacob in Padan-Aram : before Moses has been narrating the domestic life of Jacob, and all the circumstances worthy of note as to the births of his several children : now he begins to relate the way in which Jacob, having already served Laban 14 years for his two daughters and (as we learn from Gen. xxxi. 41) 6 years over, has become desirous to set up an establishment for himself, and proposes to return to his father and his own tribe, with whom, instead of being a bond-man, he would be the acknowledged heir. Laban then suggests to him, that he can become the head of an establishment of his own, without his leaving him : and, in consequence of this, Jacob agrees to keep Laban's flocks as an overseer or hind for some time longer, himself receiving a portion of Laban's cattle as the reward for his past 6 years' service (for which he has as yet received no adequate remuneration), and in order that he may be able to become a farmer for himself : he agrees to take the least valuable portion of Laban's stock as his reward, and to select from the cattle and the sheep and the goats such animals as an experienced cattle-breeder would reject. Laban, being of a suspicious nature, removes these to a distance of three days' journey from his own stock, and gives them into the hand of his sons to keep, while Jacob himself farms his uncle's estate. (Gen. xxx. 27—42.) Twenty years now pass, during which God's blessing upon Jacob is very visible—"the man increased exceedingly; and had much cattle, and maid-servants, and men-servants, and camels, and asses" (Gen. xxx. 43); but his cousins (his uncle Laban's sons) regard him with envy; and Laban, too, has acted deceitfully—he has changed Jacob's wages repeatedly. At length, Jehovah bids Jacob "Return unto the land of thy fathers and to thy kindred; and I will be with thee!" (Gen. xxxi. 3.) Jacob, thereupon consults with his wives, who at once agree to his proposals: he breaks up his camp, intending "to go to Isaac his father in the land of Canaan" (v. 18). Laban, dissatisfied at the prospect of losing such valuable services, pursues after and overtakes him, and charges him with stealing his gods. Laban searches all the tents, but cannot find the images; and then Jacob remonstrates with Laban for his conduct towards him, and says "What is my trespass? What is my sin, that thou hast so hotly pursued after me ? Whereas thou hast searched all my stuff, what hast thou found of all thy household stuff? set it here before my brethren and thy brethren, that they may judge betwixt us both. This 20 years have I been with thee : thy ewes and thy she-goats have not cast their young, and the rams of thy flock have I not eaten : that which was torn of beasts I brought not unto thee ; I bare the loss of it ; of my hand didst thou require it, whether stolen by day or stolen by night. Thus I was : in the day the drought consumed me, and the frost by night ; and my sleep departed from mine eyes. Thus have I been 20 years in thy house : I served thee 14 years for thy two daughters, and 6 years for thy cattle : and thou hast changed my wages ten times. Except the God of my father (the God of Abraham) and the fear of Isaac had been with me, surely thou hadst sent me away now empty. God hath seen mine affliction and the labor of my hands, and rebuked thee yesternight." (*V.* 36—42.)

Here two different periods of 20 years each are referred to, though expositors and chronologers have generally assumed one to be only a repetition of the other: this I proceed to shew. Whenever, in Hebrew, the demonstrative adjective זה [*Z h*] is used and repeated as a matter of contrast in the same sentence, or in two consecutive sentences ; they must be translated by "this" and "that," or "the one" and "the other," or "the latter" and "the former." Now this is the case here: the 38th verse begins with זה עשרים שנה אנכי עמך [*Z h Aasrim Shnh Anki Aam'K*] "This *period* of-twenty years, *that* I *have been* with [near] thee" (*i.e.*, the last 20 years, during which I have been your neighbour and managed your estate for you); while the 41st verse begins with זה לי עשרים שנה בביתך עבדתיך [*Z h L'I Aasrim Shnh B'Bit'K Aabdti'K*] "That *period*, for myself, of-twenty years in house thy, *that* I-served thee" (*i.e.*, the former 20 years, when I served in thy house as a bond-man). The general meaning of the whole is—that Jacob claimed to have acted uprightly throughout, twenty years as a faithful and honest servant in Laban's house, and then twenty years more as a trustworthy manager of Laban's estate; during which last period he had had continual anxiety by night as well as by day lest any thing should go wrong, and had left the management of his own property to his sons and his wives; whilst, if any thing were hurt or lost of Laban's stock, he had replaced it by some of his own cattle: and he then taxed Laban with having acted with bad faith towards him throughout, and with having changed his mode of remuneration for the services rendered no less than ten times. Laban admitted the truth of

Jacob's statement; and they then made a covenant between them, had a feast, and parted in friendship.

From all that I have previously set forth, it becomes evident, that Moses states Jacob to have lived in Padan-Aram not less than 40 (instead of 20) years; from which it results, that he was considerably younger than 77, when he first went there; and we have also a period of 33 (instead of 13) years, within which the births of Jacob's 11 sons and a daughter are to be placed: and, as Judah was his 4th son, and not improbably born within 7 or 8 years after his father's marriage to Leah, it would seem that Judah was full 25 years of age at the time of Jacob's return to Canaan. As some years elapsed after the return to Canaan, before Joseph was sold into Egypt as a slave; and as he was 22 years in Egypt, before Jacob went down thither; we have some years more than $(25 + 22 =)$ 47, as the probable age of Judah at the period of the Descent. I have thus disproved the bishop's confident assumption, that "Judah was 42 years old, according to the story, when he went down with Jacob into Egypt."

There is one point more to be cleared up before I close these remarks: it is as to the date of the narrative mentioned in Gen.

xxxviii., which the bishop claims to commence at the time of Joseph's being sold as a slave to the Midianite merchants and taken into Egypt (and, consequently, about 22 years before the Descent of Jacob). That the circumstance of Joseph's being taken into Egypt closes the 37th chapter is, of course, a fact not to be denied; but it is denied, that the 1st verse of the following chapter (the 38th) has any reference to that event. Let my previous remarks on the genius of the Hebrew language be borne in mind, and this will become apparent. In our authorised version, we read—" And it came to pass at that time that Judah went down from his brethren, and turned in to a certain Adullamite, whose name was Hirah: and Judah saw there a daughter of a certain Canaanite, whose name was Shuah; and he took her, and went in unto her." (Gen. xxxviii. 1 & 2.) We have already seen that the bishop says the words " *at that time* " must mean " after Joseph's being sold into Egypt;" but I have previously stated that Moses did not write annals. Here we have a new episode introduced into the history, which may or may not precede the one just completed. Our translators did not consider it to have any reference to the matters contained in the previous chapter, for they say " at *that* time;" whereas, had they supposed it to be connected with the previous narrative, they ought to have said " at *this* time." But a reference to the Hebrew will make all clear: the Sacred Narrative begins with the phrase ויהי בעת ההוא וירד יהודה מאת אחיו [*V'Yhy B'Aat H'Hua V'Yrd Jhudh M'At Ahhi'U*] "Now it-was in time the that, when went-down Judah from *being* with brethren his"; and the verses may, therefore, be rendered thus—"Now it happened at that time when Judah went away from his brethren and turned aside to lodge with a man an Adullamite, and his name was Hirah, that Judah saw there a daughter of a man a Canaanite,* and his name was Shuah; and he took her to wife, and went unto her." There is nothing here to shew that the circumstance may not have happened while his father was still living in Haran: all that Moses tells us is—that at some time or other Judah left his brethren for awhile, and went to live with an Adullamite; and that, while he was lodging there, he saw a woman (the daughter, probably, of a travelling merchant), to whom he took a fancy, and whom he married. There is nothing to fix the precise time when any of the events mentioned in this chapter occurred: only it is evident, that a long while intervened after the events of *v.* 1—5, before the occurrences related in *v.* 6—11; and some time must again have elapsed after the latter and before the circumstance narrated in *v.* 12—30.

---

* כנעני [*K n aa n i*] is either "a Canaanite" or "a merchant." In some of their translations of this passage, the Jews read it—"And Judah saw there the daughter of a man, a merchant."

There is nothing, then, to confine the contents of this chapter within the limits of the 22 years immediately preceding the Descent into Egypt, as they are asserted to be by the bishop; and, hence, the incredibility, which he says attaches to the story, completely disappears.

The task I had proposed to myself is now completed. I have shewn that the first of the bishop's 'prominent instances,' whereby he undertakes to prove that the Sacred Record contains 'remarkable contradictions' and involves 'plain impossibilities,' has all the characteristics of a 'true narrative of actual historical matters of fact;' and that the difficulties he has suggested arise out of the misconceptions of chronologers and the miserable bungling of expositors: whilst a logical deduction from the whole will be—that the words of Moses contain a truthful narrative of the history of the Hebrew people as to circumstances affecting the interests of the whole human race, and (as such) not unworthy of being regarded (whether considered in the whole or in its details) to have been composed under the immediate inspiration of an all-wise and merciful God. Would to God I could hope that the perusal of what I have written might cause the bishop to pause in his mad career, and soberly to reëxamine the various matters he has brought in question! My heart's desire and prayer to God for him is, that he should be saved! Oh! that he may be brought weeping to the foot of the Cross; there to acknowledge his sins, and to seek for mercy and pardon through the mediation of Him he has so despised and rejected and put to open shame—Him, who is the great Captain of our salvation—the God-man Christ Jesus! And may what I have here set forth receive the confirming testimony of the Holy Spirit to the minds and consciences of men, so far as I have been a true and faithful expositor of the words of the Divine Revelation; and unto the Father, the Word, and the Holy Spirit—ONE GOD, only Wise—the Eternal, Immortal, Invisible, yet All-seeing—the Almighty—be all the glory! Amen!

Conclusion.

In the preceding pages I have, I would fain hope, accomplished more than I originally proposed to myself, when I wrote the Preface. I must confess that I feel under one obligation (but, at the same time I must say, it is the only one) to Bishop Colenso for his publication—it is for having caused me to examine the original of the writings of Moses more than I had ever previously done, whereby I have become convinced that most of the difficulties which I had previously supposed to accompany the Sacred Narrative result from the imperfections of translations and the misapprehensions of commentators; while my previous opinion as to what has been called Biblical Chronology has been more than confirmed, for I am now thoroughly persuaded of the utter worthlessness of large portions of the usually received arrangement of the times of the events recorded in the Old Testament. If this essay shall receive the encouragement of public approval, I shall be prepared to carry the investigation further, and to examine (and, as I hope, to confute) all the bishop's remaining objections. I think I can shew that

Moses does not state the descendants of Jacob at the period of the Exodus to have amounted to 603,550 men (as stated by the bishop, and as seems to have been generally supposed), but that Moses reckons the actual Children of Israel as then being " 3,550 men from 20 years old and upward "—a number, it will be seen, less than the 4,375, which the bishop has given (at p. 111) as the result of a logarithmic calculation of the probable increase in 215 years from the 70 souls 'out of the loins of Jacob' that went into Egypt; and, as a consequence from this, that the bishop's objections about 'the size of the Court of the Tabernacle,' and as to 'Moses and Joshua addressing *all* Israel,' are without foundation: and further that Moses does not represent the Children of Israel and their 600,000 Hebrew followers as going forth from Egypt 'armed' (as the bishop says), but that they were marshalled into companies of 50 men each. I shall shew that one result of the false gloss put upon Moses's words, and the confounding of the Children of Israel with their Hebrew followers, has been to attach a weight and value to what Moses calls a ככר [*Kkr*], but which we have rendered "talent," which leads (amongst other things) to charges of absurdity upon the Sacred Writers, (1) in telling us that a crown of gold set with precious stones, of the weight of 114 lb. Troy, which had been previously worn by the king of the Ammonites, was taken off his head and set upon the head of David (2 Sam. xii. 30; 1 Chron. xx. 2); and (2) in recording that David had amassed *in his trouble* a treasure of 100,000 talents of gold and 1,000,000 talents of silver (to say nothing of brass and iron without weight, or of timber and stone), prepared for building the House of THE LORD at Jerusalem, the value of which (estimating gold at £4 per oz. and silver at 5s. per oz.) would amount to nearly £890,000,000 sterling—an amount far exceeding our own enormous National Debt, and probably a greater sum than the whole of the Coinage of the precious metals at present in circulation amongst all the Nations on the face of the whole Earth (1 Chron. xxii. 14).

While these sheets have been passing through the press, I have been gratified at the strong confirmation of my views as to the bishop's qualifications as a translator of the Scriptures, which is afforded by the valuable letters (published in "the Athenæum" of the 6th inst.) of the painstaking Anglicised German H. Heinfetter and the learned Jewish chief Rabbi Dr. Adler; and especially by the support afforded by the latter (nothwithstanding the opposing observations of "Philobiblius" in "the Athenæum" of the 13th inst.) to my translation of Gen. xxxviii. 1, confirmed by Dr. Adler's reference to Deut. x. 8.

In parting with my townsman Bishop Colenso, I can assure him, however strongly I may have expressed myself in opposition to his views, that I bear him no personal ill-will: at the same time, I must express my surprise, when I find that he, who (as a divine, to say nothing of his being a bishop of the Church of England) has declared himself to have been *called by the Holy Ghost to preach the Gospel* of the Lord Jesus Christ, should have become *an Apostle of Infidelity ;* for in no other light can I regard his 23d chapter, entitled " Concluding Remarks," when he sets the teachings of Nânuk, the Gooroo of the Sikhs, upon the same footing as the Inspiration of ' THE SON OF GOD,' and virtually says " We will not have This Man to reign over us ! " (Luke xix. 14.)

December 17th, 1862.

POSTSCRIPT.

When this work was written, I had hoped that my Answer to Bishop Colenso would have been very speedily issued to the public; and I, in consequence, wrote the preceding pages headed "Conclusion." Since then, however, I have found that there were difficulties to be overcome at the printing-office, which I had not anticipated. The arrangement of the genealogical and chronological Tables at pages 58 and 86—89, the composition of the Greek (at pages 25, 26, and 31) and the Hebrew (especially at pages 95-6), and the adjustment thereto of the representative English sounds and the corresponding English translations—have necessitated much delay; most of the Greek type and all of the Hebrew having had to be set up by my own hands, as well for the avoidance of mistakes in the composition, as also in order to the correct representation of my ideas to the eyes of the readers of my book, as I knew not where I could refer to any printed specimens of what I wanted to guide the compositor. This must be my excuse to my subscribers and the public for the seeming delay since my work was announced as being in the press.

Till my own composition shall have been issued, I have purposely avoided reading any of the Answers to the bishop which have already appeared, in order that nothing emanating from another source should tempt me to alter a sentence of what I had written; not because I am so opinionated as to suppose that I may not have fallen into any mistakes, but because I may not be chargeable with appropriating the labors of another. At the same time, I must acknowledge my obligations to two or three personal friends to whom my M.S. was submitted, for some valuable suggestions and one or two not unimportant corrections, and also to one of them (better skilled than myself in the Hebrew language) for his reëxamination of the translated passages.

The only articles I have perused that bear upon the subject are the letters which have appeared from week to week in the pages of "The Athenæum," of two of which I would here speak as being well deserving of an attentive perusal—a second letter of Dr. Adler's in the No. for the 27th ult., and a letter from J. L. Porter of Belfast in the No. for the 3d inst. : both of these supply excellent answers to some of the bishop's objections on which I have not touched.

Having read all the proof-sheets myself, I must take the responsibility of any ERRATA that may be discovered in the preceding pages ; and I, therefore, desire the reader to correct the following :—

In the Introductory matter, at p. xi., l. 15, *dele* " ve " in " devevelopment."

At p. 29, l. 12, for " of-mature-age " substitute " of-old-age (*i.e.*, of-being-a-staid-woman)."

In same page, l. 14, for "full stature" read "fullness of stature."

At p. 31, l. 11, for " this-was-happening " read " this-happened."

W. J. SPRY.

January 22d, 1863.

www.ingramcontent.com/pod-product-compliance
Lightning Source LLC
Chambersburg PA
CBHW020124170426
43199CB00009B/620